D1394784

COMPLETELY CONKERS!

summersdale

COMPLETELY CONKERS!

Copyright © Summersdale Publishers Ltd, 2009

Text contributed by Jon Stroud

All rights reserved.

Summersdale Publishers Ltd
46 West Street
Chichester
West Sussex
PO19 1RP
UK

www.summersdale.com

Printed and bound in Great Britain by CPI Mackays, Chatham

ISBN: 978-1-84953-004-0

Substantial discounts on bulk quantities of Summersdale books are available to corporations, professional associations and other organisations. For details telephone Summersdale Publishers on (+44-1243-771107), fax (+44-1243-786300) or email (nicky@summersdale.com).

COMPLETELY CONKERS!

What Drives You **NUTS** About Modern Britain

Will Jackson

Disclaimer

All stories have been researched from sources in the public domain. Every effort has been made to ensure all information and any quoted matter in these stories is correct. Should there be any omissions or errors in this respect we apologise and shall be pleased to make the appropriate amendments in any future edition. PC Sayings have been compiled from a survey conducted by jobs2view.com, which was summarised in the *Daily Express*, *The Sun* and *The Mirror*. Sexist and Non-sexist sayings have been sourced from a report by the British Sociological Association. NHS Jargon is taken from an article published in the *Daily Telegraph*.

CONTENTS

INTRODUCTION

Having a grumble is all part of being British, isn't it? We all like whingeing about the weather – one minute it's too hot, the pavements are melting and there is a hose-pipe ban in force, and the next it's too cold, the roads haven't been gritted, the railways are at a standstill and the town centre is flooded. But the thing that really gets us all going is the bureaucratic red tape that, whatever its good intentions, now ties us all up in ridiculous red knots.

It's the European Union and their decrees on bendy bananas and bagpipe music; it's the Health and Safety Executive and their madcap policies on moving office furniture; it's schools that don't allow kids to play conkers or take part in three-legged races; it's the fear of litigation that forces manufacturers to print pointless disclaimers on their products; it's the worry of being branded racist/sexist/ageist/disablist for saying the wrong thing at the wrong time to the wrong person.

It's completely conkers.

THE KIDS AREN'T ALL RIGHT

ONCE UPON A TIME, CHILDREN WALKED TO SCHOOL, PLAYED FOOTBALL IN THE PLAYGROUND AND SAT ON SANTA'S KNEE AT CHRISTMAS TIME. THINGS HAVEN'T CHANGED THAT MUCH - OR HAVE THEY?

ALLERGIC TO COMMON CONKER SENSE

There have been numerous reports of the seasonal sport of conkers being banned due to health and safety concerns – usually because of worries that an out-of-control horse chestnut might cause physical damage to person or property. An autumn can no longer pass without word of yet another school banning the activity on the pretence of protecting its pupils from hideous and disfiguring conker injuries. The head teacher of Bookwell Primary School in Cumbria went one step further, barring conkers because of the minute possibility that it could trigger reactions in children with nut allergies.

The Anaphylaxis Campaign remains completely unaware of anyone having experienced a severe reaction from exposure to conkers and branded the move an overreaction. In a stunning display of common sense, they suggested that it would be far simpler if children with nut allergies steered clear of conkery fun during break times.

THE MIND GOGGLES

Concerned that flying fragments from conkers could cause eye injuries, the head teacher of Cummersdale Primary School in Cumbria decided to take the matter of conker safety into his own hands.

Rather than impose a blanket ban on the playground pastime, he instead offered to drill holes into the conkers himself, thus ensuring that pupils would not be involved in the dangerous preparation phase. He then purchased four pairs of industrial safety goggles and ruled that children could only play at conkers on the school grounds if they donned the protective eyewear.

A SANDSTORM IN A TEACUP

Over the decades, many a child has spent an enjoyable afternoon playing in the sandpit at the local park or recreation ground. It could be a battleground for toy soldiers, a construction site for Tonka diggers and dumpers, a place to build sandcastles or even the ideal location for burying your little sister so that only her head is visible.

But things have changed. Where once the humble sandpit was de rigueur at any self-respecting playground, it's now becoming a rarity. In one survey of local authority-managed playgrounds, less than two per cent had a children's sandpit. As always, most of the authorities put the blame fairly and squarely on health and safety considerations – one even erroneously stated that playing in a sandpit could cause children to develop athlete's foot infections. The real reason these facilities are disappearing is far simpler: they cost money to maintain. Most local authorities just don't want to spend. Talk about burying your head in the sand to avoid responsibility!

BALLS OFF THE MENU

First it was salmonella from eggs, then it was mad-cow disease from beef. We're all familiar with the regular parade of media-hyped food scares plastered over our front pages. Although the risks are often incredibly small, it hasn't stopped old favourites being taken off supermarket shelves and restaurant menus throughout the country.

In the Cotswold town of Stow-on-the-Wold, however, an altogether different concern was raised regarding the inclusion of beef on the menu at the local primary school. The head teacher has banned meatballs from school dinners, believing that they could be deemed a choking hazard.

IT'S ONLY A GAME

If the media is to be believed, we now live in a shockingly aggressive society – alcohol-fuelled violence, knife crime and muggings are all, apparently, part of our everyday lives. But where did it all go wrong? Was it a slip of standards in education, the abolition of National Service or the ever-widening gap between rich and the poor? No – apparently our problems all stem from the game of musical chairs.

According to a booklet produced by the International Forum on Children and Violence – launched by Labour MP Margaret Hodge – musical chairs only rewards the fastest and the strongest and is far too aggressive a pastime for the delicate youths of today. Instead, they tell us, our children should indulge in less frenetic games and activities such as musical statues. They'll be taking their conkers away next…

CRAFTY CROCODILES FACE EGGS-TINCTION

'Right then, viewers, for today's make you'll need an empty washing up liquid bottle, a couple of toilet rolls, an egg box and a sheet of green sticky-back plastic.' Words that launched one-thousand-and-one epic *Blue Peter* craft projects. But children at an East Sussex primary school were deprived of their essential robot bodies and rocket boosters after their head teacher banned the use of egg boxes and loo rolls in craft lessons for fear of salmonella poisoning and infection.

Fortunately, after lengthy consultation with local council bosses, the situation has been cleared up and, after a seven-year absence, egg-box crocodiles and loo-roll binoculars are once again being made. Still, one question remains: where can you actually buy sticky-back plastic?

LOLLIPOP IDLE

Reinwood Community Junior School in Huddersfield prides itself as being a 'forward-thinking school where pupils, staff, governors and parents work together.' The progressive primary even has the motto, 'We always say I CAN.' This, however, proved to be in stark contrast to highways department officials at local Kirklees Council who, when asked to employ a lollipop lady to help children get across a busy road on their way to and from the school, answered with an unequivocal, 'We can't'.

For once the reason wasn't a lack of funds – quite simply it was because the road was deemed too dangerous for a lollipop lady to work safely. This, argued the parents and the pupils, was exactly the reason why a crossing patrol was needed, but the council remained adamant. Apparently, the council felt that a lollipop lady with a fluorescent jacket and a 6 ft stop sign was in more need of their protection than a bunch of traffic-dodging children.

STOP AND SEARCH

Ready to return triumphantly home with a carrier bag filled to the brim with glistening red conkers, four young lads from the West Sussex town of Littlehampton were thoroughly pleased with their afternoon's work of rummaging amongst the leaves and launching sticks at one of the town's impressive horse chestnut trees. However, by the time the seven-year-old boys made it home their bag of booty had been confiscated – in its place were four newly issued police stop-and-search forms.

Their fun-filled afternoon had been cut short by the intervention of the long arm of the law in the form of an officious WPC, who, claiming incorrectly that the tree was protected by a preservation order, confiscated their haul and issued them with the obligatory paperwork. Quite what happened to the conkers remains unclear, although the local desk sergeant is rumoured to have been seen purchasing large quantities of malt vinegar and nail varnish.

PC SAYINGS

A non-discretionary fragrance – body odour
Academic dishonesty – cheating
Cooperative physical fitness – sex
Energy efficient – switched off

ON YER BIKE

Kids, on the whole, don't get enough exercise these days. One would think, therefore, that if a child wanted to cycle to and from school each day they would be applauded as not only is it good for their health, it's also a very green way of getting about. But when a ten-year-old boy from Port Solent, Hampshire, decided to pedal his way to lessons he was told it was a big no-no – unless his mother drove behind him all the way and then took his bike home with her.

Apparently, the problem is that the road outside the school is too congested – with parents in cars dropping their kids off at the school. Of course, if the pupils were allowed and encouraged to cycle to school (like they did in the good old days) then there would be less traffic, it would be safer and there would be less pollution. But then mum wouldn't have an excuse to drive her Chelsea tractor, would she?

SPF – THAT'S SCOUT PROTECTION FACTOR

Although it has always been common knowledge that you can start a fire by rubbing together two boy scouts, the only reason you're now allowed to touch one is if he's already burnt. Strange but true… sort of.

In an attempt to circumvent any accusations of inappropriate behaviour or abuse, the Scout Association has issued a missive stating that all leaders and adult helpers are banned from applying sunscreen to any cub or scout. The restriction, however, does not apply if said cub or scout is already burnt – at this point it is considered necessary first aid. Does that qualify for a merit badge of some sort?

SUN-BLOCKED

Even a child can understand the importance of wearing a high-SPF sunscreen during the summer months. Cancer Research UK states in its guidelines that a cream or lotion of at least SPF 15 should be applied regularly throughout the day. So when a seven-year-old schoolgirl from Bury St Edmunds took a cream recommended for children with her to school on a hot July day she was surprised to be told that it was not allowed in case it caused an allergic reaction in any of her classmates. The school's official solution was… wear a hat!

THAT SINKING FEELING

Learning to swim isn't easy. There's so much to think about; pulling those arms, kicking those legs, remembering to breathe and stay afloat all at the same time. For years, kids taking their first tentative strokes have been able to benefit from numerous flotation aids such as inflatable armbands, rubber rings and foam-filled floats. But all of this is starting to change thanks to another round of health and safety legislation.

The traditional rigid, foam floats that have helped so many youngsters take to the water have been banned by many pools over fears that other swimmers could be accidentally whacked by them. Learners at other public baths have been told they can no longer make use of the inflatable rings and armbands that are normally provided free of charge due to concerns that diseases and infections could be passed on when blowing them up.

If nothing else, the additional excitement of the fear of drowning should help accelerate the learning process.

THAT'S NOT THE WAY TO DO IT

The Punch and Judy show has successfully entertained children across the land for hundreds of years; its badly behaved characters and endless opportunities for audience participation make it an enduring favourite amongst young crowds. It seemed, therefore, a wonderful idea to include such a show as part of an arts event sponsored by Newcastle City Council aimed at encouraging children to express themselves.

But no sooner had the show's performer, Bo the Clown, squeaked his first 'Huzzah!' than the red- and white-striped curtains were forced to close. The organisers had received a complaint that Mr Punch's wife- and baby-beating antics promoted domestic violence. Although when Mr Punch cries out 'That's the way to do it!', the juvenile audience shouts back 'Oh no, it isn't!' – it seems this was completely lost on the person who made the complaint. No surprises there – it later transpired that the objector had never even seen the show. That's definitely not the way to do it.

THE WRITING'S ON THE WALL FOR FOUNTAIN PENS

Handwriting is rapidly becoming a thing of the past. With computers edging their way further into everyday life, the only reason most people seem to pick up a pen is to scribble down a telephone number or scratch out some notes. It's the same in schools. Well-constructed answers have been replaced with multiple-choice tick boxes and essays are now tapped out on a keyboard rather than being crafted longhand. But it's not just technology that has caused the QWERTY generation to forgo their fountain pens; the BSI (British Standards Institute) has also played its part.

Thanks to British Standard BS 7272-1, all pens are required to have a ventilated cap – in other words, an air hole – to prevent asphyxiation should a child somehow manage to swallow it. Pens that don't have this hole, such as fountain pens, are classed as adult jewellery and have to be sold with a disclaimer stating that they are only suitable for persons over the age of fourteen years. It's nice to know that you are considered old enough to use a pen without choking at the same age you are able to apply for a firearms certificate. But then we've always known that the pen is at least mightier than the sword.

YEW'RE OUT OF HERE

Described in Jane Austen's *Northanger Abbey* as 'the finest place in England', the 650-acre Blaise Castle estate on the outskirts of Bristol is a beauty to behold; its dramatic landscape and beautiful gardens making it a popular weekend haunt for families.

The peace and tranquillity of the park, however, was somewhat rudely interrupted in the spring of 2006 when workers from Bristol City Council, the owners of the estate, were brought in to rip up a hundred young yew trees that had been planted on a site adjacent to the children's play area. This was in response to a risk assessment that considered them unsafe, because yew berries can be poisonous. Although, as was pointed out by the award-winning conservationist Trevor Beer, you would have to consume handfuls of yew berries before feeling ill.

The most insightful commentary on the situation came from local mum Helen Santry, who remarked, 'Perhaps we should drain all the lakes, chop down the trees, fill in the gorge, identify and remove any plant or fungi that is poisonous and cover the grass with cotton wool?'

YOU CAN'T HAVE YOUR CAKE AND EAT IT

What better way to celebrate your sixth birthday than to offer your friends a nice big slice of extra squidgy chocolate cake – especially if it has been specially decorated with a layer of delicious icing and a bag of chocolate buttons? That's what little Emma Matthews' parents thought when they packed their daughter off to school with her birthday treat. But her celebrations were brought to a premature end long before the cake could be divided or even a single crumb consumed when her teacher declared that, according to food hygiene regulations, the tasty sponge was a health risk as the original packaging had already been opened.

At least Emma returned home at the end of the day with the cake still intact, albeit with an attached note from the teacher informing her parents of their health and safety breach – in my day that cake would have mysteriously found its way into the staff room by mid-morning break and would be but a memory by the time the bell sounded for lessons to resume.

CRAZY DISCLAIMERS

Boots children's cough medicine – do not drive a car or operate machinery after taking this medication
Harry Potter Thunderbolt Broomstick toy – does not really fly

HAT ATTACK

It's unlikely the students of the US Navy Academy at Annapolis, Maryland, knew what they were starting when they threw their hats into the air in celebration of graduating way back in 1912. Their spontaneous action started a tradition that has been copied the world over. And what better way is there to show your joy and let off a little steam after all those exams and years of hard work? But hang on – what goes up must come down and what comes down could hurt someone. We'd better put a stop to that then!

That's the opinion of the health and safety bosses at Anglia Ruskin University, who put a stop to the practice after raising fears that the corners of errant incoming mortar boards could take a reveller's eye out. It puts a whole new spin on the idea of being injured in a mortar attack.

HO HO HO, OFF YOU GO!

With the promise of festive sweets and a gift-wrapped present, for many children (and a few adults), a trip to visit Santa's grotto at the local department store is an annual treat not to be missed. What better opportunity could there be to sit on Santa's knee and tell him face-to-beard what it is that you want in your Christmas stocking? It seems, however, that those days of knee-sitting are to be consigned to the past.

During training for its seasonal Santa staff, one London department store insists that any Father Christmas working on its premises does not 'promote or proactively seek' people to sit upon their knee and any child that does so must have been voluntarily placed there by its parents. In addition, the Santas are accompanied everywhere they go by an elf inspector [sic] to keep them in check.

One such Santa was given his marching orders after just three days into the job when a grandmother complained that she had been offended by the suggestion that she should sit on his knee. Ho, ho, ho? Bah Humbug!

But spare a thought also for our Australian cousins. Those training with the nation's largest supplier of Santa Clauses have been told to cry 'ha, ha, ha' instead of 'ho, ho, ho'. Why? Because they regard the word 'ho' as derogatory to females and fear that it could cause offence.

WHEN IS A SCHOOL NOT A SCHOOL?

Following the closure of the Watermead, Shirecliffe and Busk Meadow primary schools, a brand new £4.7 million educational establishment was built in Sheffield to serve the community. It has classrooms, teachers and 481 pupils, but it is not, however, a school. When governors were deliberating a name, they decided that the word 'school' sounded too institutional and had negative connotations. Instead, the sign at the gates welcomes you to 'Watercliffe Meadow: A Place for Learning'. The break with convention also extends to an absence of lesson bells and playground whistles and with children being encouraged to wear soft shoes indoors in an attempt to give the place a more welcoming atmosphere. It is unclear as to whether the local secondary school is likely to follow suit as 'A Place for Teenage Angst'.

NO Bs PLEASE

The head teacher of a primary school in Midlothian changed the names of two of its first year classes after some parents of pupils in 1b claimed that, although the split was purely alphabetical, it left their children feeling inferior to those placed in 1a. The classes were duly renamed 1ar and 1ap by incorporating the teachers' surnames into the new titles.

ART ATTACK

As part of a primary school art project, children were asked to paint pictures of people at work and write a short description of what they did underneath. When the artwork was displayed, a visiting school governor noticed a large number of spelling and grammar errors, and asked one of the teachers why these had not been corrected. 'So as not to discourage the children,' was the considered and caring response. The governor then noticed a single exception – the word 'fireman' had been crossed out and replaced with 'firefighter'.

ROUNDERS OUT

It was a sad day when the head teacher of Hollybrook Junior School in Southampton called a halt to thirty years of tradition by cancelling the annual staff versus pupils rounders match. The decision, taken jointly with other members of staff and the school governors, was based upon fears that the difference in physical size of the players posed a threat to the safety of the ten- and eleven-year-olds – previous encounters had, indeed, resulted in the school first-aid kit being brought out. However, on further investigation it transpired that the majority of match injuries recorded in the school accident book were, in fact, inflicted upon members of staff and not pupils. Perhaps it was all just a cunning plan to save the teachers' fragile knees and elbows from an inevitable scuffing in future games?

IT'S THE TAKING PART THAT COUNTS

According to a report presented to an annual gathering of the Professional Association of Teachers, being a failure can seriously undermine a pupil's drive and enthusiasm. Therefore, the word 'fail' should be deleted from the educational vocabulary and replaced with the term 'deferred success'. How nice it is to know that the England football team can continue to enjoy deferred success in international tournaments and that our track and field stars can celebrate deferred success at the Olympics!

WHERE'S THAT EMAIL? IT'S BEHIND YOU!

To the surprise of the organisers, an email sent by a theatre company to thirty Norfolk primary schools offering to perform a pantomime scene free in assemblies received just a single response. Curious to find out why so few schools had taken up their generous offer, phone calls were made to the schools' secretaries. Unfortunately, the pantomime's title had fallen foul of the schools' email profanity filer. But what pantomime could possibly cause such offence? *Dick Whittington!*

YO KIDS!

A training scheme backed by the government is advocating that teachers should get down with the kids and offer a hearty 'high-five' greeting to each and every one as they enter the classroom. According to the Future Leaders organisation, it's all about establishing positive relationships, which, it suggests, could inspire failing students to improve their exam results.

Have any of them actually visited a school? If there's one thing that pupils don't like, it's teachers trying to act all young, cool, trendy and 'with it'. What's going to be next on the agenda, rapping the times tables? Oh, hang on, children aren't taught those any more, are they? After all, why teach something that might actually be useful!

YOU'VE BEEN FRAMED

When staff at Edinburgh's Pirniehall Primary wanted to hang thirty pieces of art created by pupils on the school walls, it was forced dig deep into school funds and stump up £350 to pay for a professional joiner to carry out the work after health and safety rules banned staff and parents from doing it themselves. The picture-hanging ban came about over fears that if a child was injured by a falling artwork that had not been properly hung, the school or the council could be deemed liable. Prior to being displayed in the school, all of the artworks had been exhibited at a local arts centre where they were hung by a member of the school's parent council – free of charge.

DON'T BE A BAD SPORT

THE SOUND OF AN ENGLISH SUMMER AFTERNOON: THE BLISSFUL THWACK OF LEATHER ON WILLOW, CUCUMBER SANDWICHES BEING MUNCHED AND A GLORIOUS SHOUT OF 'HOWZAT!' SPORT, THE BACKBONE OF BRITISH CULTURE, MUST SURELY BE A SAFE HAVEN FROM THE HEALTH AND SAFETY POLICE...

IT'S JUST NOT CRICKET

There's nothing like the sound of leather on willow to stir the heart on a Sunday afternoon. Formed in 1840, the cricket club at Shamley Green in Surrey is reputed to be one of the oldest in the county. Its curious triangular pitch occupies a unique location and is even crossed by public roads, although tradition dictates that it's good form to either find an alternative route or at least wait for the end of an over on match days.

But, it would seem, cricket isn't everybody's cup of tea. One resident, having lived in a bungalow adjacent to the village green for less than a year, attempted to take out an injunction against the club to prevent play as he claimed that stray balls were constantly bombarding his property. Fortunately for Shamley Green Cricket Club, his request was hit for six by the local judge, who obviously thought that an English village without cricket was, well, just not cricket.

JUMPERS FOR GOALPOSTS

From Bobby Moore to David Beckham, before swapping games kit for the national strip the UK's finest footballing talent has always cut its teeth in the same way – with a lunchtime playground kick-about on a makeshift pitch. However, Burnham Grammar School in Buckinghamshire has banned the jumpers-for-goalposts tradition, declaring that flying footballs are just too dangerous, despite the fact that it boasts the country's first full-size synthetic football pitch as its star facility. Obviously, in this day and age when kids are already not getting enough exercise it's much better to sit about doing nothing on a break time.

BLINDINGLY STUPID

From football to cricket and athletics to archery, the blind and visually impaired are able to participate in a surprisingly diverse array of sporting activities. One would think, therefore, that Dudley Council should be commended for its £5,300 investment in Braille signage, which it has installed within the walls of Halesowen Leisure Centre. Well, yes – but were the signs advising of suitable footwear and on-court safety really necessary on the doors of the squash courts?

OLYMPIC AMBITION

In his time, hurdler Peter Hildreth was quite an athlete. He represented Great Britain at three Olympics (Helsinki in 1952, Melbourne in 1956 and Rome in 1960), won a bronze medal at the 1950 European Championships and, on five separate occasions, equalled the national 100 m record with a time of 14.3 seconds.

With the arrival of his eightieth birthday in 2008, Mr Hildreth was keen to see if he was still made of the same sturdy stuff that had propelled him to hurdling fame some fifty years before. Part of his original training regime had been to head down to the depths of the London Underground and sprint the wrong way up the escalators. There are no tube stations where he lives in the Surrey town of Farnham, but there is a multi-floor department store – Elphicks. Despite his advanced years, the grandfather of five still managed to power his way up the shop's moving staircase in record time, but on this occasion, rather than being met with an invitation to represent his country at the 2012 Olympics he was confronted by an irate store manager in the lingerie department.

Apparently, enough octogenarian customers fall over on the store's escalators going the right way that the thought of one going in the wrong direction was a little too much to bear. For once, health and safety considerations may have a point and, just to be sure, Mr Hildreth has been told that if he tries it again he'll receive a ban – probably one that the Court of Arbitration for Sport won't be taking up on his behalf.

PC SAYINGS

Uniquely coordinated – clumsy
Uniquely proficient – incompetent
Under-attractive – ugly
Over under-attractive – uglier
Over under-attractively gifted – ugliest

RAIN STOPS PLAY

Most people would agree when it comes to swimming that the presence of water is essential. After all, without a liberal quantity of the stuff, rather than swimming you would be dragging yourself along the ground – what's more, diving would probably just result in the need for a bucket and mop and a trip to the local A & E. But safety chiefs at Hackney Council think that it's possible to have too much of a good thing.

Staff at the council-owned London Fields Lido in the borough declared that it was unsafe to swim there after a brief rain shower. Their justification was that the conditions would impair visibility for their lifeguards, making it hard for them to see if anyone was in trouble in the water. This might have been understandable had it been monsoon season in Rangoon, but perhaps not in the case of a light spring shower in London.

WEEING WHEELERS STOP RACE

The internationally ranked Havant Grand Prix cycle race with its tough and uncompromising 113-mile course over the South Downs had, over the years, attracted many riders from across the globe. From Olympic hopefuls to enthusiastic amateurs, it had seen them all. The popular race, however, suffered a premature demise in 2006 when it was banned after a stalemate developed between organisers and the police over concerns that competitors might attempt to make use of the Hampshire roadside hedgerows as a convenient place to relieve their bladders. A statement from the Hampshire Constabulary proclaimed it was 'unacceptable to have masses of cyclists at the side of the road urinating' and the race was stopped on the grounds of maintaining public safety. What exactly are they putting in those energy drinks?

RAFTERS UP THE CREEK

The River Rother Raft Race not only serves as a tasty tongue-twister, but has also raised a considerable amount of money for local charities. Those taking part frantically paddle the length of the four-mile course from Cowdray Ruins in Midhurst to Lods Bridge in Selham aboard all manner of questionable home-made maritime craft. But despite the crafty rafters having enjoyed an unblemished twenty-six-year safety record (save for a single wasp sting that required hospital treatment), red tape and regulations have made the competitors' aquatic endeavours all the more difficult to organise.

To control the 500-strong crowd that would line the four miles of riverbank – that's an average of one spectator every 25 m if you take both banks into account – the organisers were instructed to produce an Event Safety Management Plan including a detailed risk assessment, a communications plan, an emergency plan and a 'hierarchical structure of safety responsibility'. This last demand was, perhaps, the easiest to satisfy as the hierarchical structure of the River Rother Raft Race was comprised of just two people.

NORWICH SAYS 'BEAT IT' TO MP3S

Many of the participants at the City of Norwich half-marathon found their usual running routine turned upside down when organisers banned them from listening to personal MP3 players whilst taking part. For many athletes, from novices to experienced runners, listening to an uplifting tune while covering the miles is part and parcel of their formula for success – it can concentrate the mind and help time pass more quickly. But health and safety officials claim that people who listen to pounding beats whilst pounding the tarmac are a danger to themselves and to others. It would seem that with earphones attached sensible runners are just not capable of keeping to the side of the road or spotting fluorescent-jacketed marshals at junctions and turns. Quite how a few disco beats can have such a serious effect on your vision and motor skills is unclear although, it has to be said, looking at your average club-goer could give the theory some credence.

No Fun and Games

A satisfying game of conkers, a trip to the local bonfire night celebrations and a stunning firework display to light up the inky blue night sky - a perfect November's evening or just another health and safety nightmare?

AVAST ME HEARTIES!

'Avast, ye scallywags, and lay down yer weapons, arrrrgh!' came the cry from West Country officials on discovering that organisers of the Carnon Downs Drama Group in Perranwell, Cornwall, were using a deadly array of swords and firearms in their amateur production of *Robinson Crusoe*. Well, deadly might be overstating it a little – the swords were made of plastic and the guns did nothing more than fire a flag emblazoned with the word 'BANG'.

To their amazement, the group were instructed to first and foremost contact their local police station to have all of the weapons checked for safety. They were then told that, when not in use, the whole cache of arms must be kept in a safe-box which, in turn, must be stored in a locked room.

It's lucky they weren't performing *Peter Pan* – heaven knows what the health and safety regulations are regarding crocodiles.

BARBIE BAN

Which of us hasn't popped along to the local summer fete and enjoyed a carbonised sausage or burger covered in onions and ketchup wrapped up in a fresh bun, all provided, of course, by the local Rotarians/scout troop/village hall fund/cricket club (delete as appropriate)? Not only is it all usually exceptional value but it also supports the community both financially and in spirit. Risk-averse Camden Council, however, doesn't quite see it that way and have declared that professional caterers must be brought in to run any coal barbeques on their patch. And don't think for one minute that a quick switch to other fuels will satisfy the north London safety police – those operating gas cookers at these events will be required to participate in a council-run course to gain a special qualification. Anybody for salad?

CLOWNING ABOUT

The smell of the greasepaint, the roar of the crowd – the circus might once have been an exciting place to visit but health and safety at work regulations imposed by our friends in Brussels seem to be doing their best to take the fun away from the funambulist (that's tightrope walker to you and me).

Goussein Khamdoulaev has been a circus high-wire performer for over twenty years and has performed the world over as part of the Moscow State Circus. His act involves death-defying somersaults performed on a wire some 50 ft above the heads of his audience – all without the aid of a safety net. But, funnily enough, it's not the lack of a net that has caused a stir; it's his choice of headgear – a traditional rabbit fur Cossack hat – which, say the EU bureaucrats, just won't protect him if he were to make an unplanned gravity-assisted descent to the arena floor. Instead, he has been ordered to wear a hard-shell safety helmet. Is that really going to make that much of a difference? As they say, it's not the fall that hurts; it's the landing that follows!

It's not just Mr Khamdoulaev who's fallen foul of the big top safety police. His comedy colleague, Valerik Kashkin, has been told that he can no longer clown about in his madcap size eighteen boots for fear that he too might injure himself. Next they'll want to send the exploding clown car for a mandatory MOT each year.

COME ON AND DO THE CONGER

The Dorset seaside resort of Lyme Regis is celebrated for a number of reasons. It was once the home of Mary Anning, a famous nineteenth-century palaeontologist and fossil collector whose Jurassic discoveries delight countless children to this day. The Cobb, the town's distinctive harbour wall, found fame when a black-cloaked Meryl Streep stood upon it whilst staring out to sea as the waves crashed around her in the film *The French Lieutenant's Woman*.

Less well known is the town's unique sport of Conger Cuddling – essentially a game of human skittles in which the pins are members of the Royal National Lifeboat Institution. The human pins are dressed in oilskins and stand on upturned flowerpots, and the ball (which in no way resembles a ball) is a 5 ft-long, dead conger eel attached to a rope. For years it had kept townsfolk and visitors amused and had raised considerable funds for the lifesaving charity.

Unfortunately, the annual event has become yet another victim of our politically correct culture. Just a single complaint from an animal rights group forced RNLI bosses to call an end to the fundraising fun. Apparently, dead conger eels have feelings, too.

IT'S NOT ALL CONKERS

In recent years, the game of conkers has been the subject of much scrutiny and, for those that like to indulge in a spot of horse chestnut warfare, this has, on the whole, been rather unwelcome. The phrase of choice for those implementing a conker ban is, of course, health and safety. Organisers of the World Conker Championships, held in the exotic climes of Northamptonshire, were therefore rather surprised when a new sponsor stepped forward ready and willing to put its name to the annual international extravaganza – the Institute of Occupational Safety and Health.

Fed up with getting the blame for health and safety decisions being enforced in the realm of conkers by people with little or no real knowledge of such matters, the Institute felt that enough was enough and decided to get string-deep into the action. Not only has it become the competition's official sponsor, its staff have actually taken part as Team IOSH and the IOSH Bonkers, joining competitors from as far afield as Brazil, Jamaica and the Philippines. You don't have to be conkers to work there, but it helps.

IT'S THE MONKEY BY A NOSE

If you've ever frequented one of Britain's countless horse-racing venues, you may well have heard the phrase 'betting a monkey'. For the uninitiated, this simply means that some confident punter is happily waging £500 of his hard-earned cash on the outcome of a race. However, travel to the Welsh seaside resort of Llandudno in the summer and you might hear of someone actually betting *on* a monkey!

For thirty-nine years, the highlight of the town's annual fun day on Bodafon Fields has been an enjoyable donkey derby in which a dozen or so grinning children were mounted on the animals and led at a steady canter by experienced handlers in a dash to the finish line. But now those smiling children are consigned to the sidelines as insurers, fearful of costly litigation, say that, despite there not having been a single injury in the event's long history, it's all just too dangerous for them to take part. In their place ride a phalanx of blow-up sheep and one soft toy orang-utan – a late replacement after one of the air-filled ovines failed to remain inflated.

What's next – hard hats and high-visibility jackets when constructing sandcastles?

MAGIC DRAGON PUFFED OUT

Once upon a time, in a lovely big children's book, there lived a big pink dragon. The dragon tried ever so hard to do the right thing and wanted so much to be loved but he couldn't ride on the back of the witch's broomstick, he upset the beautiful princess by getting muddy paw prints over her pretty dress and he scared the brave knight, who made him run away. But those were the least of his worries for he had upset someone even more important – the health and safety officer.

One thing we all know about dragons is their ability to breathe fire. It would appear that while it is perfectly acceptable to belch flames when doing battle with a fearsome adversary, it's not a satisfactory method for one to toast some marshmallows.

Incredibly this is no fairy tale. Lindsey Gardiner, an author and illustrator with fifteen books to her name, was told to lose the dragon's fire-breathing episode from her artworks when her publisher considered it too dangerous. In a previous book she had already been instructed to change a picture of a boy on a ladder as her editors considered it to be 'precarious' and were worried they could be sued by a parent should a child try to emulate his actions.

Does this mean that the three little pigs need to be issued safety helmets and that Jack needs to take working-at-heights training before he can climb his beanstalk?

MONKEY MADNESS

An organ grinder from Matlock in Derbyshire found himself and his monkey banned from the streets of Ripley after local council licensing bosses decided that he needed to complete a risk assessment of his activities, detailing all possible hazards and how they could be made safe. It's not even as if the monkey, named Simon, was in danger of jumping up and attacking somebody as it was, in fact, just a battery-operated toy. The worst it could do would be to demand a banana at an inconvenient moment.

Simon's woes were not the first to befall the streets of the Derbyshire town. Shortly before his ban, a similar fate was bestowed upon a troop of dancers and a Punch and Judy show. All three acts had been hired by the town council to entertain shoppers but each and every one was deemed a risk to public safety.

There's an example of forward planning at its best.

LOCAL AUTHORITY JARGON

Across-the-piece – everyone working together
Area focused – concentrating on just one thing
Best practice – the right way to do something
Bottom-up – based on ordinary members of the public

NO KNICKERS, PLEASE

If there's one pastime you'd associate with the fans of Wales's favourite ballad-belting son, it's knicker throwing. Quite simply, any appearance of the great Sir Thomas Jones Woodward OBE is not complete without an aerial bombardment of lingerie. Someone else who knows all about this is Tom Jones impersonator Simon Abbotts, whose doppelgänger performances are also subject to an accompaniment of airborne underwear. But when Mr Abbotts came to make an appearance on primetime Saturday night television show, *The One and Only*, so concerned were BBC bosses that their pseudo-Tom would come a cropper on an errant undergarment they insisted that pant flinging was to be an absolute no-no. Why, why, why?

NUTS GRABBED BY COUNCIL KILLJOYS

The perfect conker is a delight to behold. It should be decent size and shape, possess a core as hard as steel and be wrapped in a slightly springy outer shell with the kind of satisfying glossy sheen that would have pleased the late Arthur Negus had he found it resplendent on a fine antique sideboard. But top quality conkers don't grow on trees – well, not if Newcastle City Council has anything to do with it!

Worried by the potential damage to property and the life-and-limb risks taken by tree climbers in the search for the ultimate sixer, workers from the council's environmental services team were despatched to remove all the conkers from dozens of the city's horse chestnut trees before Geordie youths could get anywhere near them. They must be nuts!

OUT-GUNNED BY THE SAFETY POLICE

Branded a child-eater and one who 'feared neither God nor man', Sir Thomas Lunsford was the most terrifying of all Royalist commanders during the English Civil War.

Lunsford led a colourful life. 'A swaggering ruffian', as a young man he was once indicted for attempted murder. Captured by Roundheads at the Battle of Edgehill, he was imprisoned in Warwick Castle for two years. He rejoined the Royalist army following a prisoner exchange but was again captured at the siege of Hereford in 1645, resulting in further incarceration in the Tower of London for three years. It is, however, fair to assume that Lunsford never had to deal with the most formidable of all adversaries – a health and safety officer. This joy was left to his spiritual descendents – the members of Sir Thomas Lunsford's Regiment of Foote, a division of the modern-day English Civil War Society.

When the regiment was asked to take part in a historical re-enactment at the Clarke Hall Educational Museum near Wakefield, a local council official (a Roundhead sympathiser perhaps?) ordered a ban on the firing of gunpowder, suggesting that the Royalist musketeers shout 'bang!' instead. When asked to explain its action, the council professed it was all in the interests of public safety and to protect nearby windows.

At least the pikemen weren't forced to wear high-visibility breastplates!

SHHHH... IT'S THE LAST NIGHT OF THE PROMS!

Whether it's the booming cannon of the *1812 Overture* or the crashing cymbals during the final refrain of 'Land of Hope and Glory', everyone knows that the traditional Last Night of the

Proms at London's Royal Albert Hall is a noisy affair. This annual excuse for a bit of flag waving to a patriotic soundtrack has been with us since 1895 and has always served to stir the heart. But, thanks to an EU directive on sound levels in the workplace, the whole thing is set to become an altogether quieter experience.

To protect sensitive eardrums, sections of the orchestra must now be separated on different levels and even have sound-deflecting screens placed between them – perish the thought that some poor flautist should be subjected to the bass tones of a tuba or shrill blast of a cornet disturbing their earwax. Rehearsal times have also been cut and technicians, crew and even the musicians themselves are now required to wear earplugs at all times.

As if all that wasn't enough to pour cold water in a musician's trumpet, should the whole performance exceed 85 decibels then lights will flash and the orchestra will be asked to quieten down its performance.

STRICTLY HEALTH AND SAFETY

There are a number of things required for ballroom dancing – grace, poise and timing to name but a few. Another essential is a nice highly polished floor upon which partners may glide as if floating on air. Blackpool, with its tea dances in the Tower Ballroom and competitions at the Empress, has enjoyed a long tradition of accommodating the dancing public. But sadly, some of the town's smaller community venues are facing a bleak future. In a move that would see Bruno Tonioli and Craig

Revel Horwood clutching at their sequinned trousers, town council health and safety inspectors have ordered that their gleaming parquet floors be covered over with carpet – just in case someone should slip over and hurt themselves.

As far as Blackpool's ballroom fraternity are concerned, this is akin to concreting over the pitch at Wembley or laying turf at Silverstone and, far from preventing injuries, could actually cause more. According to the chief executive of Blackpool Coastal Housing, the local council department responsible, he is 'aware it is not perfect for dancing, but it is perfect for karate'. Strictly kung fu anybody?

THAT'S ALL FOLKS!

They've electrocuted each other, thrown knives at each other, blown each other up with dynamite, attacked each other with various tools and garden implements and have even been known to drop the odd Steinway on each other. No, we're not talking about the Labour Party backbenchers; we're talking about Tom and Jerry, the cartoon duo who, for the best part of seventy years, have been able to get away with pretty much anything without raising the hackles of a single health and safety inspector. But while their overtly violent antics have pretty much escaped scrutiny, certain other aspects of their lifestyle have not.

In 2006, Ofcom, the independent regulator for the UK communication industry, received a number of complaints about two cartoons – *Tennis Chumps* and *Texas Tom*. In the first of these Tom's caddish tennis opponent is seen smoking a huge Cuban cigar while in the latter it's Tom himself who is seen puffing on a cigarette in an attempt to impress the ladies. As a result, all scenes in Tom and Jerry cartoons in which smoking appeared to be condoned were told 'That's all folks!' and edited out.

TOO COLD TO DIP

Taking an early morning dip in ice-cold water is not everybody's idea of how best to see in the New Year but, from Brighton beach to the Firth of Forth, it's a celebrated tradition supported by hundreds of brave souls. At one such event held at Lee Dam Reservoir near Todmorden, West Yorkshire, those of a suitably hardy constitution have, for the past fifty years, competed for a commemorative trophy. With separate races for men, women, boys and girls, the event has regularly attracted over fifty swimmers.

But now, despite providing emergency scuba divers and canoeists, the organisers have been forced to call it a day as a change of terms means that their event is no longer covered by the Amateur Swimming Association's insurers and the cost of taking out an alternative policy is prohibitively high.

There is, however, one form of salvation for those who prefer their aquatic activities served ice cold – the National Cold Water Swimming Championships. Tooting Bec Lido in south London holds the annual races where the water temperature can plunge to as little as 3°C – cold enough to freeze the flippers off a penguin.

THE GLOWING RESORT

Whether watching from the roadside or actually taking part, for twenty years residents of the little Cornish fishing port of Looe were able to enjoy one of the great spectacles the south-west of England had to offer – the traditional torchlight procession organised every year in the run-up to Christmas. As many as 500 people would gather before filing along the town's narrow streets with blazing torches in hand to congregate at the Rose Gardens for some carol singing.

Although the event had passed for two decades without incident, concerns were raised by the harbour authority and the council that the risk of fire was becoming too great. Their solution, while managing to keep the streets aglow, was far from illuminating – the traditional flaming torches were replaced with 500 plastic glow sticks of the sort used on camping trips, turning the parade into something more akin to the entrance queue at an illegal rave.

THE BONFIRE STRIKES BACK

Frustrated at the mountains of paperwork, endless health and safety forms and new council regulations that created a need for additional marshals, the organisers of Ilfracombe Rugby Club's annual Guy Fawkes Night firework display and bonfire struck upon a novel idea to ensure that their popular evening would pass without accident or concern. Although the fireworks spectacular remained unchanged, rather than go down the traditional route of building a huge pyre from old pallets and timber offcuts they hung an enormous 22 ft by 15 ft screen between the goalposts onto which was projected a movie of a previously filmed bonfire in all its raging glory. To really add to the effect, industrial heaters were positioned under the screen to warm the audience. Apart from a few watchers being disappointed that their marshmallows failed to toast, the whole event was a blazing success.

Someone needs to tell the organisers of the Bonfire Night at Watford's Cassiobury Park of this inventive solution, because, after thirty-eight years, the local council has banned its annual bonfire as it no longer complies with the town's smoke-free policy.

REMEMBER, REMEMBER

You would think that, if there was one safe place to put a bonfire, it would be right next door to a fire station – especially if it had been built by the firefighters themselves. Not according to council health and safety inspectors in Coleshill, Warwickshire. The station's annual Guy Fawkes celebrations were called off as a result of new legislation requiring all public bonfires to be kept secure and monitored twenty-four hours a day, seven days a week, from the moment they begin pyre construction. With the enormous Coleshill bonfire taking many days to construct it was just an impossible demand. What hope is there for the rest of us if even the fire crews can't be trusted with a box of matches?

Local Authority Jargon

CAA (comprehensive area assessment) – assessing local services

Cardboard citizen – homeless person

Core message – the main point

Coterminosity – all singing from the same hymn sheet

SAY 'NO' TO FIR!

What better centrepiece for a town or village's festive decor is there than a splendidly decorated Christmas tree? Standing tall and proud they are seen the length and breadth of the nation at yuletide, and bring delight to shoppers young and old. That's if you can actually get close enough to see one.

In Anstruther, on Scotland's east coast, a health and safety review by the local council has resulted in the village Christmas tree being encased by a ring of steel. The risk assessment – which even took into account the potential weight of perching seagulls – proclaimed that a diminutive 10 ft fir tree was all that could be deemed safe. As if that wasn't enough, officials encased the base of the trunk in concrete before surrounding it with orange and white traffic barriers and then encircling it with an 8 ft-high metal security fence.

'Tis the season to be jolly!

BELT UP SANTA!

Every twelve months, for one single night, he travels millions of miles from rooftop to rooftop. Since time *in memoriam* he has managed this astounding feat without need of ABS, satnav or parking sensors. All in all he's got a pretty unblemished driving record. Unfortunately, however, a clean licence and enviable no-claims bonus is not enough to satisfy certain elf and safety officials – in Halesowen, Santa is now required to a wear a seatbelt.

Though the Halesowen and Rowley Regis Rotary Club's charity Santa sleigh only reaches a maximum cruising speed of just 5 mph while being towed by a Land Rover, its occupants must clunk-click every trip thanks to demands from insurers paranoid of litigation should Father Christmas take a tumble. The solution was a specially constructed harness – extra large to accommodate his mince-pie-enhanced waistline.

Next they'll be demanding that Santa declares his sleigh as SORN for six months of each year.

THEY'RE BEHIND YOU!

From the Theatre Royal to the local village hall, the traditional Christmas panto is as much a part of the festive tradition as fairy lights, *The Great Escape* and plum pudding. But even this great institution is under threat from health and safety regulations put in place to allegedly save us all from our own stupidity.

In one amateur production of *Jack and the Beanstalk*, Jack was informed that he was permitted to climb up to a maximum height of just 4 ft from the ground and then only if he were fitted with an approved safety harness. At another theatre, *Peter Pan* was grounded after it was decided that a full structural survey of the premises would be required before the go-ahead would be given to install roof brackets for his flying wires. Sweets, which were customarily thrown into the audience for eager children to catch, now have to be lowered from the edge of the stage for ushers to hand out in a controlled manner.

Look out for those health and safety inspectors – they're behind you!

HAPPY GLOWMAS

Church records are renowned for being incredibly accurate. They are, for example, an invaluable source of information in tracking down one's ancestors or when undertaking historical research. The records at Chelmsford Cathedral are no exception – births, deaths and marriages are all there, as are details of the damage to the cathedral's roof and windows during the civil war in 1641, the collapse of the nave in 1800 and the dedication of a window to the United States Air Force in 1953. One thing that does appear to be missing is any reference to any church-goers having gone up in flames during the annual Christingle service since its inception in 1747.

But unfortunately for those now taking part, a 250-year-old unblemished safety record is no longer good enough to satisfy the health and safety police. Gone are the evocative candles secured onto festively decorated oranges – in their place are bright, but thoroughly artificial, fluorescent glow sticks. What's going to be next – strip-lighting around the altar?

ANIMATED OPERA

During a production of *The Marriage of Figaro* at Newcastle's Theatre Royal, opera-goers were transfixed by an additional member of the cast – a woman dressed in black who stood at the corner of the stage and proceeded to sign the entire performance for the hard of hearing. A regular feature of productions by the national company Opera North, she must have been extremely fit and dextrous to manage the final chorus!

BLUE EXPECTS...

Lord Nelson's victory over the combined French and Spanish fleets off Cape Trafalgar in 1805 is rightfully considered Britain's greatest naval triumph. It resulted, of course, in the demise of the Admiral – shot down at 50 ft by a French marksman aboard the *Redoutable* – but proved to be a pivotal point in the campaign against Napoleon.

In commemoration, the summer of 2005 was marked with a series of events under the banner of Trafalgar 200. The highlight of which was an International Fleet Review of 167 vessels in the Solent followed by a re-enactment of the Battle of Trafalgar itself. Well, sort of. Instead of the might of the British fleet taking on French and Spanish ships, political correctness stepped in, making it a battle between the reds and the blues, lest our continental cousins take offence.

No one was less impressed by, and more critical of, the situation than seventy-five-year-old Anna Tribe from Monmouthshire – Lord Nelson's great-great-great-granddaughter. She described the mock battle as 'pretty stupid' and commented that such a politically correct attitude would 'make fools of us'.

'I am sure the French and Spanish are adult enough to appreciate we did win the battle,' she added.

FIVE GET POLITICALLY CORRECT

Enid Blyton's creations have thrilled generations of young readers. From *The Adventures of Noddy* to *The Secret Seven* and *Malory Towers* to *The Famous Five*, there's something for any youngster who cares to glance between the covers. But even these classic works of children's literature are not safe from the politically correct ink of the editor's pen, with many of the characters, situations and language being altered to suit modern tastes and considerations.

The gender division between the boys and girls of *The Famous Five* and *The Secret Seven* have been consigned to a dusty leather 1940s suitcase and pushed firmly under the bed. Now all of the characters participate in each other's activities – boys doing household chores and girls playing rough. Quite where that leaves poor old George, nobody can be sure. Julian will no longer declare 'I say, that's a bit queer' at the start of every chapter. Instead a change of accent and inflection sees him uttering a rather bland 'Hey, that's odd.'

In the *Adventurous Four* series, Jill and Mary have been changed to Pippa and Zoe to bring them up to date while Fanny and Dick of the *Faraway Tree* stories have been renamed Frannie and Rick. Dame Slap, meanwhile, a character famed for giving naughty children a deserved smack, has been transformed into Dame Snap who now only offers a damn good telling off!

Unfortunately, because these are books aimed at children, publishers seem to feel that they have the right to change them at will to suit their middle-of-the-road politically correct agenda. Nobody seems quite so keen to rework the creations of Jane Austen or Charles Dickens.

Driving You Round the Bend

Whether you are navigating a one-way system in your car, negotiating a country lane on your bike, or letting the train take the strain, travelling from A to B was never going to be easy.

SIGN OF THE TIMES

Road signs are popping up all over the place. Where once we might have been allowed to use a little common sense, we are now subjected to a bombardment of painted aluminium road furniture telling us how, what, where, when and why. Few places offer a more impressive visual assault than Low Street in the North Yorkshire village of South Milford where, in the space of just half a mile, drivers are subjected to an intimidating total of forty-five road signs advising of roundabouts, footpaths, cycle lanes, speed limits and a whole miscellany of other hazards. Yet according to the RAC, most people can only manage to keep track of about five pieces of information at any one time. So with a new sign flashing past every 1.3 seconds, how exactly is a driver supposed to have any time to concentrate on the road ahead?

TOTALLY TROLLIED

Lots of jokes have been made over the years about the little tartan shopping trolleys wheeled around by those of a certain age on trips to the supermarket. However, a great-grandmother from Lydney failed to see the funny side when a bus driver in the Forest of Dean banned her from his service because he considered her little plaid wonder to be a potential obstruction and a health and safety hazard. Forced to walk over a mile home up a steep hill, she was in so much pain when she got home that she had to visit the doctor the following morning.

Challenged about their driver's action, operator Stagecoach was unrepentant, stating that 'The buses on that route are not designed for shopping trolleys or pushchairs.' How nice to see them showing so much concern for one of their elderly customers.

UNDERGROUND ARTWORKS

If you happen to be travelling on the Tube in London, keep a sharp eye out for some rather unusual warning signs. Health and safety's answer to Banksy has been out and about with a collection of stickers that, to the casual observer, look just like legitimate Transport for London notices – pay a little more attention, however, and you soon realise that there's more to their message than meets the eye. Do the signs over the doors actually say 'naughty passengers will be crushed' and is there really a fine of £200 for talking? At peak hours is it an absolute necessity that one allows others to sit on their lap and does the Northern Line really do a loop-the-loop between Clapham Common and Clapham South?

The ultimate instruction: iPods must be worn at all times. If you don't have an iPod then play with your phone, read a newspaper or pretend to be asleep.

GIVEN THE BRUSH OFF

There are a number of things that will get you kicked off the number 9 bus from Cardiff's Heath Hospital to Prospect

Place – abusive language, carrying an offensive weapon or scrawling graffiti on the windows will all suffice; so will being in possession of a tin of paint from the local DIY store. As discovered by seventy-three-year-old grandfather Brian Heale when he attempted to travel with the 'antique cream' emulsion he needed for a spot of decorating at home.

According to health and safety regulations governing public transport, paint is listed as a hazardous material and may only be taken on board a bus if it is carried in two containers – for example, a sealed pot within a plastic carrier bag – and must not be left unattended or in a place where it might slip or slide.

Fortunately for Mr Heale, after being ejected from the bus (thankfully not while it was in motion) he and his paint were given a lift home by a local cafe owner. There's nothing like a cup of tea to inject a little common sense into a situation.

COLLI YSTYR WRTH GYFIEITHU – LOST IN TRANSLATION

When the local authorities in Swansea received reports of lorries using a quiet residential road to access a supermarket for deliveries, they quickly came up with a straightforward solution: they would install a road sign to bar unwanted traffic. But as all official road signs in Wales are required to be bilingual, council officials first needed to email their in-house translation service for guidance.

When the reply promptly came back, no time was wasted in producing the appropriate large sign and getting it displayed at the roadside:

'No entry for heavy goods vehicles. Residential site only / *Nid wyf yn y swyddfa ar hyn o bryd. Anfonwch unrhyw waith i'w gyfieithu*'.

At first it appeared that the problem was solved but then calls started coming in from Welsh-speaking members of the public, all of whom were more than a little confused by the instructions they were being given.

Perhaps 'I am not in the office at the moment. Send any work to be translated' isn't what you would expect to see displayed by the roadside on a 6 ft by 4 ft metal sign.

It's not, however, just Swansea that gets things wrong in the translation department. When workers from the Vale of Glamorgan Council put up a temporary sign between Penarth and Cardiff advising cyclists to dismount at a set of roadworks they had no idea that the Welsh translation – *llid y bledren dymchwelyd* – actually read as 'bladder inflammation upset'.

Another sign in Cardiff advised English-speaking pedestrians to 'Look Right' whilst instructing Welsh-speakers to 'Look Left'.

'*Ymddirheurwn am unrhyw anghyfleustra a achosir yn ystod gwaith adnewyddu*', however, is a perfect Welsh translation of 'We apologise for any inconvenience caused during refurbishment works.' It's a shame that the sign bearing these words was placed on building works in the Bridge of Don – a suburb to the north of Aberdeen located some 270 miles from the nearest patch of Welsh soil.

PARKING PANDEMONIUM

Chaos ensued on Main Street in the Lancashire town of Kirkby Lonsdale after a council blunder resulted in conflicting parking restriction signs being displayed. Although one sign correctly informed drivers that there was to be no parking between 8 a.m. and 6 p.m. seven days a week, another sign, just yards away, announced that restrictions would only apply between 9 a.m. and 6 p.m. from Monday to Saturday. As a result, traffic wardens were unable to issue any tickets or even move motorists on at any time of the day on any day of the week until the signage issue was resolved.

You would think that it would only take a couple of screwdrivers and an ounce of common sense to knock this problem on the head, but no… South Lakeland District Council might well have been responsible for enforcing parking regulations but it was the highways department of Cumbria County Council that was in charge of erecting, removing and altering road signs.

IT'S NOT ROCKET SIGNS

You would think that so-called professional drivers would have a pretty good grasp of the Highway Code. Road signs, at the very least, should be a doddle for those who spend their working lives behind the wheel, but this turned out not to be the case in the sunny seaside city of Brighton.

For some time the junction at Trafalgar Street had been marked with a simple 'No entry' sign but, after the introduction of a cycle lane, it was replaced with a different one – a car and a motorbike on a white circle with a red border. There's no ambiguity as to the meaning of this sign – it means no motor vehicles.

Now perhaps the driver of an articulated lorry, who carried on up the street in spite of the sign, thought his vehicle was powered by fairy dust and not diesel. Whatever the reason, the upshot of his actions was to leave his HGV and its load of bricks well and truly wedged under the bridge next to Brighton station, causing the road to be closed for four hours. It's fair to say that the same weird logic might also have influenced the coach driver who ploughed into the same low bridge a week later, inflicting more than a little distress on a party of school children, who had been looking forward to a day out at the local Sea Life centre.

Incredibly, both of the drivers blamed the 'confusing signs' and not their own stupidity for their actions. Their stance was even backed up by the local GMB Union representative, who felt that there should have been consultation with the local taxi and bus trade before the changes to the sign were made.

Worried that further accidents might occur, the council subsequently changed the signs back to the original 'No entry' ones. One question remains – does this mean that any pedal pushers making use of the cycle lane will now be breaking the law by going past the sign? According to the Highway Code they will!

FARCE CLASS FARES

Once upon a time, when you wanted to travel on a train, you popped along to the local ticket office, told the nice chap with the peaked cap and impressive moustache where you wanted to go and he'd look it up in a big thick book and tell you how much it was going to cost. No messing about, no silly games – the only options were whether you were travelling first- or second-class and whether or not you were travelling at peak times.

Now it seems the possibilities are not only endless but also, on the whole, incredibly pointless. One survey estimates that there are now approximately 350 different types of ticket to choose from with the official fares manual having grown from a lightweight half-dozen pages in the 1980s to a whopping 202-page tome today.

A simple journey from London to Glasgow can flag up as many as forty-five ticketing options on countless routes through a whole gamut of different operators from National Express and Virgin to ScotRail. But it's not just the multitude of routes and ticket types that are there to catch you out – there's also the issue of the rather arcane set of terms and conditions that accompany them.

When Eric Vose needed to make a business trip from Newcastle to London, he purchased an advance first-class ticket using his senior railcard for the princely sum of £45.85, for which he was allocated a reserved seat in coach L, seat number 13A. However, a last-minute family emergency led to him deciding instead to join the same train at Durham, some fifteen miles further south.

But when Mr Vose arrived at the ticket barrier in Durham, he was told that his ticket wasn't valid as he hadn't joined the train at Newcastle. He explained the situation to no avail and, with great reluctance, was forced to pay an additional £66.65 for a single fare south. Just to rub salt into the wound, he spent his journey in – yes, you've guessed it – coach L, seat number 13A – the very seat he had already paid for in advance.

LOCAL AUTHORITY JARGON

Cross-cutting – working together
Cross-fertilisation – the spreading of ideas
Distorts spending priorities – uses up cash

CONNEX CHAOS

If a rail company announced that over the course of a year it had cancelled forty-nine trains, missed 276 stations, caused eighty hours of delays for commuters and had been unable to assist in a Transport Police investigation of a death due to a lack of drivers, you would think that it was a pretty poor display of management and ability. Incredibly, this catalogue of errors tells only part of the story of a single day in the life of the short-lived rail operator Connex South Central – the network that, until the rails were pulled out from underneath them in 2001, was in charge of providing services to the packed commuter routes in Sussex, Surrey, Kent, Hampshire and Dorset.

On that same day, only thirty per cent of all scheduled services had actually run on time, several drivers failed to show up for work or turned up late, ten busy commuter trains were sent out with only four carriages instead of the correct eight, causing hundreds of passengers to stand during their hour-long journeys, several trains broke down, one train couldn't depart on its journey because it had no conductor while another service from Victoria to Gatwick was signalled to start but went nowhere as it had no driver on board. The situation was so bad at Horsham that Connex had to pay for taxis to take stranded customers to their destinations.

Come the evening rush hour, over twenty trains were cancelled due to a further lack of drivers, a signalling failure on the East Sussex coast caused twenty-one hours of delays and another problem in Surrey resulted in eight hours of delays.

When quizzed about the problems, managers at Connex insisted that safety was their greatest priority. Fair enough, but you would have thought that getting your passengers from A to B might have been up there somewhere.

THE KISS NOW ARRIVING ON PLATFORM 4

If David Lean's cinematic masterpiece *Brief Encounter* were to be set in modern-day Warrington rather than wartime Carnforth, it would have to take on an entirely different storyline – Laura and Alec would be busily ushered to a designated kissing area for their emotional farewell, so as not to delay all those busy commuters rushing to make their way to catch the 5:40 on platform 4.

Warrington Bank Quay was the first railway station in the country to put up no-kissing signs on its concourse, platforms and taxi rank. The designated 'kissing zone' has been allocated in a corner of the car park, although even this has detractors as it slows traffic during peak times. It remains to be seen what the penalty fare is for having an illicit snog in the waiting room.

SILLY IN SCILLY

Sitting in the Atlantic Ocean, twenty-eight miles off the coast of Cornwall, the Isles of Scilly are a remote corner of the British Isles. Incredibly, the hilltop airport servicing the archipelago is the tenth busiest in the UK, with a large amount of freight and in excess of 140,000 passengers passing through every year.

The job of air traffic controller on the island is, therefore, of significant importance. Wherever they are working, all controllers are highly trained and are required to adhere to a stringent set of internationally agreed standards, including regular medical checks and an eye test. The work itself involves being able to clearly communicate with incoming and outgoing air traffic, monitoring of ground-based radar and the visual identification and guidance of aircraft coming in to land. At the Isles of Scilly airport on St Mary's, all of this has to happen on what is often a windy or fogbound runway.

Odd, therefore, that when the Council of the Isles of Scilly placed an advertisement for a fourth air traffic controller the application form was offered in both Braille and audio format.

APOSTROPHES BANNED

Fed up with valuable staff time being wasted fielding letters, emails and telephone calls from an army of pedants, Birmingham City Council has, once and for all, banned apostrophes on all its street signs. Kings Heath is no longer King's Heath (or Kings' Heath for that matter) while Queens Drive will be forever lacking its possessive.

In an age when schools across the nation are desperately trying to teach correct spelling and punctuation it begs the question: why didn't they just get it right in the first place? That, however, just opens a whole new can of worms from people with too much time on their hands who will happily argue until they are blue in the face that, as Kings Heath or Kings Norton are no longer the property of the Crown it is grammatically correct not to include an apostrophe.

At the other end of the spectrum, and thankfully not within the jurisdiction of Birmingham City Council, is the village of Westward Ho! Nestled comfortably on the north Devon coast between Bideford and Bude, this seaside resort has the only place name in the United Kingdom that includes an exclamation mark.

LOST LUGGAGE

If you've ever taken a flight and realised that while you're standing next to baggage carousel G at Stansted Airport your luggage is probably circulating on carousel C at Charles de Gaulle, you'll understand the frustration caused by late and lost luggage. But how big is the problem?

The Air Transport Users Council estimates that, in the world each year, around forty-two million bags are mishandled with just over a million of those never being returned to their rightful owners. According to the British Airports Authority, thirty-six per cent of misplaced bags are the result of delayed flights, twenty-three per cent are caused by loading delays, while thirty-two per cent are a consequence of unloading delays and another six per cent due to problems with handling. We are left to imagine how the other three per cent (that's 1.26 million bags) are misappropriated. Alien abduction perhaps?

T5 TURMOIL

It was supposed to be the jewel in the British Airways crown – a £4 billion construction project lasting nineteen years and capable of handling twenty-five million air passengers a year. However, on opening, it soon became apparent that all was not well at Heathrow Airport's state-of-the-art Terminal 5.

Within the first day alone, thirty-four international flights were cancelled and the baggage checking-in system was suspended. In the days that followed, over 500 flights were cancelled and

28,000 items of luggage were caught in a huge backlog. To get back on track, lorry loads of luggage were transported 600 miles by road to Milan for faster sorting and distribution by a courier company. In total the fiasco is thought to have cost British Airways somewhere in the region of £50 million in lost revenue and compensation claims.

DOUBLE YELLOW LI...

Double yellow lines at the roadside are, on the whole, a necessary evil. After all, with the levels of traffic now on our roads, their absence would herald untold chaos in our towns and city centres. You do, however, have to question the thought process that led to the positioning of some of the nation's parking restrictions.

Norwich, for example, has a stretch of double-yellows running for just 24 in (60 cm) on Theatre Street and another running for a paltry 36 in (90 cm) on St Stephen's Street. Smart cars are small but it would have to be a 'genius' car to fit into a space that tiny. Forget the fact that not a single car in the history of motoring could actually squeeze into one of these places without the help of a scrapyard compactor – the law is the law and it says that you're not allowed to park there… even if you could. Clear? These Norwich micro-spaces are, however, nothing compared to an example found in the nation's capital where a single yellow line restricts parking on a whole 18 in (45 cm) of Highbury Crescent in Islington.

MIDDLE-LANE MADNESS

If there's one thing guaranteed to get the blood boiling on a motorway journey it's middle-lane drivers – those blissfully unaware and supremely inconsiderate individuals who can't manage to fathom the basics of the Highway Code and would rather sit at the head of a mile-long bottleneck than risk the shame and indignity of being seen as a slow-lane driver.

Aware of the problems caused by this antisocial attitude to driving, the Highways Agency has tried to be proactive by installing 'Don't hog the middle lane' signs on several motorways. While this is generally to be applauded, one can't help but question the logic of one such sign situated on the M54 in Shropshire – after all, this motorway only has two lanes.

LOCAL AUTHORITY JARGON

Double devolution – empowering people

Early win – getting something right

Flexibilities and freedoms – having the power to do the right thing

Horizon scanning – looking for warnings of potential problems

DON'T BLAME IT ON THE BOOGIE

Under new legislation proposed by the Department for Transport, 'every description of watercraft' will be subjected to a new set of laws concerning 'safety, conduct endangering ships, structures or individuals and drugs and alcohol offences.' Fair enough if you're talking about car ferries and super-tankers or even speed boats and sailing craft, but the same legislation is also to be imposed upon boogie boards, body boards, sailboards, kite-surfing boards, canoes, kayaks and dinghies. Even those with little nautical knowledge, with perhaps the notable exception of the DfT, can see that a boogie board bears little resemblance in size, shape, purpose or speed to a powerboat or container ship. Before we know it they will be reclassifying prams, pushchairs and skateboards into the same category as articulated lorries and coaches.

VIRGIN ON THE RIDICULOUS

After spending two weeks competing at various locations across Europe with his 6 ft kayak, a seventeen-year-old schoolboy and GB junior men's freestyle team member, Tom Turner, was left high and dry on the final leg of his journey after jobsworth Virgin Trains staff at Milton Keynes Central stopped him from boarding his train. To add insult to injury he was told he was not even allowed to stay inside the station as he waited to be collected as his kayak posed a health and safety risk.

Tom had already travelled by train to Milton Keynes from Luton Airport and had intended to travel on to Preston and home. Instead, he had to endure a four-hour wait in the pouring rain while his parents drove the 170 miles from Skipton, North Yorkshire, to collect him. He finally got home at 2 a.m. the following morning.

All things considered, it might have been quicker and easier if Tom had just paddled his way home.

CARRY ON CONUNDRUM

When taking a flight, there are lots of things you're not allowed to carry in your hand luggage – axes, hatchets, arrows, darts, ice-picks, machetes and meat cleavers all make the list, as do baseball bats, knuckledusters and coshes. Why is it, then, that it's perfectly permissible to walk into an airport duty-free shop and buy a couple of two-litre bottles of Russian vodka, a silk scarf and a disposable lighter – the perfect ingredients for a Molotov cocktail?

IN THE SHITTERTON

Satnav is a wonderful invention. After years of making do with a ten-year-old AA road atlas and a selection of illegible notes and hieroglyphs scrawled on scraps of paper masquerading as directions we all, at last, have access to a fairly accurate (although not entirely foolproof) method of finding our way from A to B. That is unless you're after directions to

Shitterton – a hamlet just off the A31 to the west of Bere Regis in Dorset.

It seems that for the satnav manufacturers – and for that matter the major online mapping services – this very real place name is too rude to contemplate putting into their systems. Even that bastion of cartographic excellence, Ordnance Survey, did their best at wiping the little village off the map when, in 2006, its 1:50,000 series map had it marked as 'Sitterton' – a name which, it should be said, is favoured by certain more prudish members of the local community and the local water company which has defiantly labelled its local sewage pumping station as its Sitterton facility. The OS, thankfully, saw the light and corrected further editions but the village still has to put up with other inconveniences – not least the repeated theft of the sign announcing that you have arrived in Shitterton.

Whether you would mind living in a place called Shitterton or not, spare a thought also for the residents of the following unfortunately named places:

Thong – appropriately located near Shorne in Kent
Twatt – nestled up on the Shetland Islands
Slutshole Lane – Besthorpe, Norfolk
Hardon Road – Wolverhampton
Bonks Hill – Sawbridgeworth, Hertfordshire
Busty View – Chester le Street
Fanny Hands Lane – Ludford, Market Rasen, Lincolnshire
Fingrinhoe – near Colchester, Essex
Lower Pleasure Gardens – Bournemouth, Dorset

WHAT IT MEANS TO BE GREEN

RECYCLE, LEAVE THE CAR AT HOME, USE LESS OF THIS, USE MORE OF THAT – WE'RE ALWAYS BEING TOLD THE IMPORTANCE OF ADOPTING A LEAN, GREEN LIFESTYLE. BUT BEING GREEN WOULD BE SO MUCH EASIER IF IT WASN'T FOR ALL OF THAT RESTRICTING RED TAPE.

A BLOW FOR WIND POWER

The world's natural resources are a valuable commodity and not to be wasted – all the more reason why in recent years it has been important to embrace alternative renewable energy sources. Once considered little more than a novelty, wind turbines are becoming a more common sight in our countryside and on our coastline.

When the thirty-turbine North Hoyle Offshore Wind Farm was opened in 2003, five miles off the North Wales coast, it was heralded by the then prime minister, Tony Blair, as a 'highly significant step towards achieving Britain's renewables goal.' What a shame that within months of everything being switched on it was all being switched off again. The reason? It was too windy.

ALL POWERED UP AND NOWHERE TO GO

In our energy-conscious nation, we are forever being told to act green, conserve power and turn off those lights when we're not using them. It's common sense really. No wonder, then, that the residents of the Scottish town of Dalkeith became a little bemused when they discovered that a local high school was remaining illuminated at night. A wasteful approach at the best of times but the red brick buildings of Dalkeith High School had long been abandoned and left derelict!

So why the unnecessary drain on the national grid? Surely this must be some kind of mistake; a simple timer set in the wrong position, a mischievous young lad playing silly games? Not at all! The lights were being left on, at the taxpayers' expense, by Midlothian Council to ensure that when thieves and vandals break in, they don't hurt themselves by tripping over furniture or falling down the stairs.

Perish the thought that some poor miscreant should find himself in Dalkeith A & E!

BARROW BAN

Andre Wheeler, a design and technology teacher from the Leicestershire village of Barwell, likes to do his bit for the environment; for eight years he has been recycling as much as he can – paper, cardboard, glass, tin cans, plastic cartons and garden waste. And he doesn't leave it there; rather than cause more environmental damage by driving to the local tip (sorry, household waste and recycling centre) he loads everything into his wheelbarrow and spends ten minutes walking it there. Or at least he did…

Concerned about the safety of Mr Wheeler walking onto the site and its own staff should he manage to plough one of them down, Leicestershire County Council banned the barrow, insisting that if he wished to use the facility he'd have to drive there and back.

Want to be green? Get a car! Somebody should also remind the council that a third of all car accidents happen within a mile from home.

FLAGGED DOWN

Some members of society have a need or desire to travel incognito from time to time. Whether it is for speed, privacy or security, travelling below the public radar is a skill and an art which often takes time, planning and a great deal of organisation. The mayor of Maidstone, however, seems to be doing a remarkable job at doing this thanks to the efforts of the council's own health and safety department.

In years gone by, the mayor's arrival was easy to observe – the first citizen being chauffeured to civic events in a rather smart, dark blue Jaguar complete with distinctive number plate, mayoral crest and bonnet-mounted flag bearing the town's coat of arms. But times move on and, in an attempt to appear green, the Jag has been replaced by an altogether more inconspicuous and fuel conscious Lexus GS450 hybrid. Now there's nothing wrong with the Lexus – it's a very stylish-looking car that is more than commensurate with the job in hand – it's just that the town's democratic services manager (that's a new one on me) says that it will have to go without its crest and traditional flag – just in case the 8 in by 5 in (approximately 20 cm by 12 cm) rectangle of cloth happens to fall off and damage a car or inconvenience other road users.

LEFT HIGH AND DRY

If there is one artist whose paintings define early nineteenth-century English rural life, it must surely be John Constable.

But the very landscape he made famous in masterpieces like *Dedham Mill* and *The Hay Wain* has come under threat from an unlikely source. No, it's not a new bypass or industrial estate, nor is it some intrusive form of factory farming or a virulent crop disease. The problem comes from the Environment Agency.

Following an accident in which one of its employees injured his arm whilst opening a floodgate, the Environment Agency took an unprecedented unilateral decision to cease operating eighteen cast iron mill sluices on the Stour, Blackwater and Colne rivers in Essex and Suffolk – rivers which have had their levels artificially managed for over 1,000 years. By leaving the sluices closed they have all but emptied some eighteen miles of the Stour, which has, in turn, impacted on the region's fragile ecosystem and several endangered species that inhabit the area. Of more concern to many local residents is the worry that, with the gates permanently closed, there is an increased risk of flooding should the area be subjected to exceptionally heavy or prolonged rainfall. The Environment Agency says that this is unlikely, but then look at what happened to Gloucestershire in 2007 when the whole county ground to a halt and thousands were left without power or drinking water.

It's truly amazing how a millennium of careful water level management can be ousted with a simple cross of a safety inspector's biro. Surely threatening a Constable is a criminal offence?

THE LADY WITH THE BICYCLE LAMP

She saved her employers something in the region of £1,000 a year in petrol costs, was a familiar face in the community and was able to keep fit in the process. All a glowing commendation for district nurse Kathy Archer who cycled anything up to fifteen miles a day on her rounds rather than use a car. But Bournemouth Primary Care Trust has now branded her green and pleasant mode of transport as inappropriate and a risk to her safety and that of others, stating that it left her open to attack from drug users and could increase the danger of spreading infection – claims which the Royal College of Nursing branded as nonsense. Unfortunately for Mrs Archer, she is now confined to four wheels and has to spend a proportion of her day trying to find a parking space instead of just locking up at each of her calls.

LOCAL AUTHORITY JARGON

Improving levers – tools to get the job done
Innovative capacity – the ability to come up with ideas
Lowlights – what they got wrong
Menu of options – choices

TOO GREEN TO BE SEEN

When a community wins a civic award such as 'Best Kept Village' or 'Cleanest Town' it's usually a cause for celebration. The groundskeepers from Test Valley Borough Council were, therefore, overjoyed to discover that Memorial Park in Romsey had been granted a Green Flag Award by the Civic Trust. In recognition of this honour, the council decided it would be a wonderful idea to erect a flagpole from which the pennant could be displayed.

Unfortunately, the council's own planning department saw things rather differently, deciding that a flagpole would be an inappropriate addition; instead, they recommended the installation of a plaque… to commemorate the awarding of the flag.

SCAMPI TALES

Next time you settle down for a tasty platter of scampi and chips, consider for a minute the epic journey that your breaded seafood snack has undergone to make it as far as your plate. Although British langoustines are generally caught in the Irish Sea and off the west coast of Scotland, those produced for Young's Seafood have a high-mileage round trip to do before they make it to the kitchen of your local pub eatery.

Rather than being prepared at a factory locally, once caught they are quickly frozen, packed into refrigerated containers maintained at -26°C and sent off on a 6,500-mile, twenty-one-day sea journey to Thailand where they are shelled by hand before being frozen once again and reshipped another 6,500 miles back to bonnie Scotland. Only then are the tails breaded and bagged as Young's Scottish Island Scampi.

YOU MUST BEE JOKING!

When a gardener from Ystrad Mynach in Wales contacted his local council for permission to relocate two beehives from his home to an allotment plot, he found the response incredible. The official from Caerphilly Borough Council told him that he would have to put a dab of paint on each and every one of the 50,000 bees so that he could be identified as the owner should anybody get stung. Ouch!

WOOD GATHERING AXED

Created by the barons of England in 1215 to limit the powers of the renegade King John, the Magna Carta became the bedrock upon which our citizens' rights were based. Of these rights, some have long been consigned to the history books while others, in one form or another, have survived to this day. Estovers, from the Old French *estovoir*, meaning 'that which is necessary', gave tenants the right to take fallen timber from common land to use in fence making, tools, for home repairs and as firewood. It was this right that, for twelve years, retired builder and Betws-y-Coed resident Mike Kamp exercised within Gwydyr Forest by means of a special licence granted by Forestry Commission Wales.

But, despite the fact that people have collected their own firewood the world over since time *in memoriam*, the Welsh Forestry Commission's health and safety 'experts' have now deemed it far too dangerous and have axed the 800-year-old tradition. This in an age when we are all being told that we need to do our bit to help protect the world's natural resources.

If common sense falls in a forest while nobody is there, does it make a sound?

In the Interests of
Public Safety

With the everyday hazards of falling into your local duck pond or being struck by ripe pears as they fall from trees, it's good to know that the council remains one step ahead when it comes to protecting us from these and other very serious dangers. In fact it's amazing that we even venture outside our front doors, especially with those unwelcoming welcome mats just waiting to trip us up!

THE BOTTOM OF THE PROBLEM

According to health and safety legislation, if a seat is anything less than 17.75 in (45 cm) from the ground, the buttocks of infirm people are below the point at which they can comfortably return to a standing position. For this reason, Bramcote Crematorium in Nottinghamshire was instructed to replace forty memorial benches, at a cost of £400 each, following a visit by a tape-measure-wielding bottom inspector from Broxtowe Council.

At just 14.75 in (37 cm) from ground to cheek, a derriere placed on a Bramcote bench was in grave danger of remaining planted for all eternity.

EALING ARBORICIDE

Ealing Councillors found themselves at the centre of controversy after it was revealed they were considering felling 4,500 mature lime trees across the borough. The 100 ft trees were planted in Victorian and Edwardian times and are a distinctive and popular feature of the borough but the council maintained that their £55,000 annual maintenance bill (about £12 per tree) was too costly and that the trees caused subsidence and damage to pavements. In a grasp at redemption, the council insisted that for every tree they cut down they would plant two new saplings, but with Tree Council research proving that ninety-three per cent of trees planted in an urban setting die from neglect within five years, their argument was proven to be nothing but dead wood.

All of which is rather ironic when you consider that Ealing Borough Council's logo is a tall and proud tree.

KILLER PEARS FROM ON HIGH

St John's Villas in Archway is a pleasant little corner of the busy metropolis that is London. One of its most notable features has always been the impressive leafy rows of pear trees that line the kerbside. Sadly, for many years, these wonderful trees were the victims of neglect by the local council until, in 2005, they were on the receiving end of a trimming session that was more crew-cut than a little off the top.

Curiously, this brutal bout of pruning had a bizarre side effect – a bumper crop of gigantic perry pears the following year. Unsurprisingly, many residents were delighted by the trees' remarkable fruity offspring. Health and safety officials from Islington Council, however, had different thoughts on the situation.

Worried that an errant fruit might land on a passing pedestrian or cause damage to a parked car, they branded the pears a danger to the public and ordered the trees to be chopped down. Locals were quick to point out that the copious crop was only a result of the council's own work. Some residents even offered to pay for the fruit to be picked rather than see the trees lost forever but Islington Council said no, citing the fact that the trees were theirs and theirs alone.

It would be interesting to learn how many people are injured each year from falling fruit!

MOVING THE GOALPOSTS

The joys of a countryside stroll might well include admiring the landscape, spying unusual birds in flight, examining a rare wild flower or watching a lone deer as it breaks cover. All in all it is a highly visual experience. Funny, then, that Cheshire County Council's rights-of-way inspectors saw fit to have a pair of white, waist-high children's goalposts situated in a field crossed by a public footpath removed, for fear that they might constitute a hazard to walkers at night – apparently, nobody seemed aware that after-dark rambling was such a popular past time in Alderley Edge.

ONE IN THE EYE FOR COMMON SENSE

Being able to see where you're going in the local swimming pool would seem a good idea to most. Not so the health and safety brigade. According to boffins at the British Association of Advisors and Lecturers in Physical Education, wearing swimming goggles poses a real risk to children as the eyewear could, if first pulled away from the face, snap back and cause an injury. Those in the know seem to think it better that the young blindly run the gauntlet of flailing arms and kicking legs than see clearly where they are heading.

Age, however, is no barrier to having goggles metaphorically snapped in your face, as Londoner Roland Grimm found out when he tried to go for his regular dip at the local baths in Swiss Cottage, where for the last thirty years he had happily swum wearing a scuba-diving mask. He liked its design because, not only did it prevent water going up his nostrils, its one-piece plastic glass didn't press hard against his face. But, according to centre management, this type of mask is a liability as it could cause breathing difficulties and restrict vision. It's alarming to think about the grave danger three million people who scuba dive worldwide put themselves in just by donning their masks.

LOCAL AUTHORITY JARGON

Place shaping – creating environments where people can thrive

Predictors of beaconicity – factors that would lead to a local authority being rewarded

Provider vehicles – local authority vehicles

Resource allocation – money going to the right place

POND LIFE

The pond at West Itchenor has been a feature of this pretty West Sussex village for centuries. Over the years, people have fished there, children have collected newts and frogspawn from its waters and families have sat nearby feeding breadcrumbs to the waiting ducks. But now, thanks to local council health and safety experts and much to the disbelief of villagers who have enjoyed its peace and tranquillity, this archetypal scene of rural bliss has been classified as a water hazard and, despite having an unblemished safety record, now requires fencing along one side and signs warning of deep water. Now are they sure that they don't need a lifeguard?

SAFETY MAT-TERS

It's polite to wipe your feet before entering someone's home – especially if there's foul weather outside. But Bristol City Council have other ideas about the presence of the humble welcome mat and have banned the household item from all communal areas in its flats and high-rise blocks as a potential trip hazard. Thousands of residents were sent a specially prepared letter titled 'Health & Safety Issues – Hazardous Mats' notifying them that they should remove the offending articles immediately or face confiscation. What's next? Door knockers banned in case someone traps a finger?

TALK TO THE PALM

What would you expect to see from a Torquay hotel room? Sydney Opera House? Herds of wildebeest sweeping majestically across the plains? Unlikely. But, even Basil Fawlty would have recognised the palm trees that, over the years, have become such a distinctive feature of what is known as the English Riviera. These palms, however, which even feature on the region's official emblem, have, as the result of a town centre risk assessment study, become the unlikely centre of attention for council health and safety officials who believe that their sharp, pointed leaves pose a potential hazard to passers-by. Planners are now required to bear in mind that 'palms need to be carefully and appropriately used' and ensure that future plantings are kept out of harm's way.

WARNING - FLOWERS AHEAD!

With its thatched roofs and climbing roses in abundance, the Wiltshire village of Urchfont has a picture-postcard beauty. This is a place that is obviously well cared-for by its residents, to the point that, in 2005, it won the title of Best Kept Village in Wiltshire. Over the past eight years, no one has been more dedicated to maintaining its appearance than June Turnbull.

The public flower beds in the village have become a labour of love for this enthusiastic pensioner, who is often to be seen grubby-fingered with trowel in hand, tending to their needs. Even those unversed in horticultural matters could see that she has done a fantastic job, all of which has been paid for out of her own not-so-deep pockets.

Wiltshire County Council, however, are a little less impressed – according to their inspector, Mrs Turnbull is required to apply for a licence under Section 96 of the Highways Act 1980. Furthermore, June has been instructed that if she wishes to carry out any further roadside gardening she must wear a fluorescent jacket, set up three metal signs to warn motor vehicles of her activities and also employ a lookout to warn her of any danger.

SNOW JOKE

Despite being known as the 'Fair City', Perth in Scotland sees more than its fair share of inclement weather. As we all know, a blanket of wet leaves can make things pretty slippery underfoot, as can a covering of snow. Residents of two sheltered housing complexes in the town didn't, therefore, think it too unreasonable a request to ask for assistance from the local council in clearing their walkways and paths. To their shock and surprise the answer was a resounding 'no'. Baffled residents were informed that if a path was cleared by the council and somebody was subsequently injured, the council could be held liable and sued. If, however, the path was not cleared and someone fell and was injured, the council could not be held responsible.

Incredibly, several of the residents did actually fall and receive minor injuries but there was nothing whatsoever that they could do about it.

WATCH WHERE YOU WALK

We're always being told to be careful and to watch how we go. Health and safety officials consider even the most incongruous items risks to our security. In a country where doormats can be considered trip hazards and even firefighters are banned from using stepladders, it seems as if nothing can be taken for granted. One of the most phenomenally stupid pieces of design must, therefore, be the 'pedestrian deterrent' paving finding its way into the urban landscape.

Constructed of uneven granite slabs and often with sharp, protruding edges it is supposed to put off walkers from straying from marked pathways. But the crazy thing is that if a regular pavement was laid that offered the prospect of upending innocent members of the public it would be ripped up and removed in an instant as a risk to life and limb. You might just as well embed broken glass into the concrete.

LOCAL AUTHORITY JARGON

Scoping – working something out
Service delivery failure – failing to empty your wheelie bin
Third sector – charities and voluntary organisations
Worklessness – unemployed

STAIR CRAZY

It cost the residents and the owners of a caravan park in Beeston Regis, Norfolk, over £50,000 to build and had been used by hundreds of people without incident or injury. However, after just three weeks of use, a professionally built wooden staircase that allowed holidaymakers to safely make their way down a 100 ft sandy cliff to a pleasant little beach was shut down after North Norfolk Council's environmental health managers declared it too steep to comply with current regulations, following a complaint from a single resident of the 270-caravan site. As a result, the lower section of the stairs has had to be rebuilt, costing an additional £8,000. For the sake of a couple of degrees the whole thing is just stair crazy.

THE BUILDING BLOCK SOCIETY THAT LIKES TO SAY 'NO'

Trying to keep the kids entertained during a shopping trip into town is not the easiest of tasks – boredom and pester power are effective weapons for the under fives. What a relief it is, then, to be able to deposit the youngsters in front of a big box of Lego while you patiently wait your turn in the queue at the bank. For many years, this had been one of the benefits of banking with the Saffron Building Society, but health and safety concerns now mean that the ever-popular building bricks are now consigned to the manager's office. One might think their concern would have been based on the slim possibility that someone's little treasure might end up swallowing a small plastic chimney pot or the wheel of a racing car – after all, in these cash-strapped times the Saffron wouldn't want to go killing off potential customers no matter how young they might be – but no. Their concerns were based around the even more miniscule chance that one of their existing customers might trip or slip on a pre-schooler's masterpiece of construction and end up suing the society for damages.

In the meantime, we have to wonder what the branch managers of the Saffron Building Society have been doing with all those spare bits of Lego.

TRENCH FOOT AND PAPER CUTS

Swindon author Mark Sutton spent three years meticulously researching his book, *Tell Them of Us*, a detailed account of the daring deeds performed by the town's brave sons during those perilous days of World War One. Courageous they may have been, but their exposure to constant shelling, gas attacks and the horrors of trench warfare paled into insignificance compared to Sutton's own plight – his battle with Swindon Town Council.

For the seemingly simple task of selling the book in the local tourist information office they were demanding that he took out a £5 million public liability insurance policy. Why? The local authority were concerned that some poor soul might just drop a copy of his book on their foot or get a paper cut from its pages and sue. Unsurprisingly, Mr Sutton told them where they could put their policy – something to do with Arras, apparently.

BALLOONY DECISION

There are many reasons that could prompt a security guard to bar a customer from entering a store; the individual might be known to them as a shoplifter, or they could have been seen acting suspiciously outside. The store might even have a 'no hoodies' policy. But when a nine-year-old girl was blocked from entering her local supermarket with her mother, it wasn't because she had a juvenile-law-breaking past or that she'd committed a crime against fashion – it was because she was clutching a helium-filled balloon given to her by staff at a local restaurant where she had enjoyed a family lunch. Staff at the store explained that if she were to unintentionally let go of the balloon it could possibly float up to the ceiling and interfere with the shop sprinkler system – that meant the balloon was a risk to customer health and safety. Who had they been talking to? Richard Branson?

SURVEY UNDER WRAPS

Concerned that you or I might do mortal damage while opening our morning carton of orange juice or box of Wheatie Puffs, the Department of Trade and Industry instigated a comprehensive study on the difficulties of opening modern packaging. Employing an extensive team of academics and consultants and costing £100,000 of taxpayers' money, it left no crisp packet unturned. The final report was a page-turning sensation, not least for its bombshell of a conclusion that 'the larger the area for grasping, the more force that can be applied to open a package'. What a triumph of scholarly insight.

CROSS WIRES

It's a natural desire to protect one's property, so after four break-ins in the space of eighteen months, the family of a ninety-three-year-old Northampton resident thought it prudent to string up a length of barbed wire around the perimeter of her garden and along the back of her bungalow accommodation. For the first time in years she felt safe and sound in her own home. For two years the wire did an admirable job as thieves no longer considered her home an easy target; you might say that the wire acted as a deterrent. That was until local council officials decided to have their say and ordered it to be taken down – just in case anybody tried to climb over it and got injured in the process. Do you think they will be asking the Queen to do the same thing at Buckingham Palace?

WHO'S BIN DOING YOU A DISSERVICE?

THEY'RE PAID FOR BY YOUR COUNCIL TAX; THOSE GREAT BIG WHEELIE BINS THAT CLUTTER THE STREETS OF GREAT BRITAIN, LOOKING LIKE AN ARMY OF DALEKS. SURELY YOUR LOCAL COUNCIL REFUSE COLLECTION SERVICE ISN'T TIED UP IN YARDS (SORRY, METRES) OF BUREAUCRATIC RED TAPE?

A RUBBISH COLLECTION

Nobody likes to pay council tax, but we all have to. One would justifiably think that if you pay upwards of £2,000 a year, you can expect a certain level of service to come as standard. Rubbish collection, for example.

Lancashire's Ribble Valley Borough Council seems to have other ideas. They have now issued residents in certain areas with 360-litre communal bins. Not too much of a problem if, for example, you live in a small cul-de-sac within the environs of a town but potentially a bit of a bind if you live right out in the sticks.

For eighty-year-old Bolton-by-Bowland resident June Kay, this has meant dragging the huge communal bin the length of her driveway and back – a round trip of a mile – every week, negotiating on the way a very steep hill, livestock and a cattle grid. The bin, which is shared with her neighbours and another couple who live over two miles away, can't be left at the end of the lane because it obstructs farm traffic and could easily roll into the unlit country lane and cause an accident.

Unrepentant, Ribble Valley Borough Council claims that it had to find the 'most effective system' that could 'work within the budgets' – apparently they had to do so regardless of the impact it would have on their taxpaying residents!

A WEIGHTY PROBLEM

When dustmen stuck a 'too heavy to move' sticker on Katie Shergold's garden waste recycling bin she thought it a bit odd.

She had, after all, managed to wheel the bin of grass cuttings from her garden round to the front of the house without any difficulties whatsoever and left it just 6 ft from where the West Wiltshire District Council dustcart had pulled up. 'If we can't pull your wheelie bin with two fingers it's too heavy' was the statement from the digitally challenged bin men.

Suffice to say that certain West Wiltshire residents have their own two-fingered response when it comes to dealing with the local council's waste collection policies.

CHIP AND BIN

Endorsed by the government and managed by South Norfolk District Council, the only thing that a pay-as-you-throw waste scheme achieved was to successfully dispose of £1.2 million of the taxpayers' money.

Launched in 2005, the project involved the distribution of special microchipped wheelie bins to 52,000 households and the installation of a £25,000 scanning and weighing system on to each of the council's twelve refuse trucks. When working properly, the hi-tech trucks were supposed to weigh each bin six times as it was lifted for emptying and then six times as it was lowered. The weight of the rubbish along with the residents' details from the microchip were then supposed to be logged in an on-board computer fitted in the cab. That's when it was working properly…

Bin men found themselves being turned into hydraulic technicians and IT experts as the system constantly failed and needed running repairs to allow them to complete their rounds.

The final nail in the coffin was a 250 per cent increase in local fly-tipping.

Thankfully, a newly elected council saw fit to consign the scheme to the scrapheap!

CONTAMINATION ALERT

The word contamination can bring some scary images to mind – Chernobyl, Torre Canyon, Bhopal… the Somerset Waste Partnership.

So what is it that could have caused such a case for consternation from these West Country recyclers? A devious conglomerate pumping chemicals into the atmosphere over Yeovil? Unauthorised dismantling of nuclear weapons in Taunton? A super-tanker that has run aground off Minehead? No, it's two 10 inch-square (25 sq cm) pieces of turf in Karen Kelly's garden waste wheelie bin.

One would think that if anything constituted garden waste it would be a couple of oddments of turf. After all, in most people's gardens the lawn takes up the majority of the space. Think again. Mrs Kelly was informed that, as it could not be composted, the soil attached to the grass is considered a contaminant, and that her bin wouldn't be emptied until the offending objects had been removed.

Does this mean that the whole of the British countryside is contaminated?

PC SAYINGS

Mortgage-free living – homeless
Sexually focussed, chronologically gifted male
individual – dirty old man
Street activity index – crime rate

KERB SIDE STORY

Remember the days when the bin men used to cheerily whistle their way down your garden path, pick up that old metal dustbin, hoist it over their shoulder and carry it out to the waiting dustcart for collection? It all seemed so simple. These days dustmen – sorry, that should be 'refuse collection operatives' – are wrapped up in so much red tape and bureaucracy that the whole process is more rubbish than the content of the bins they (occasionally) empty.

Mark Birkett lives in Hilperton, Wiltshire. For years he had dragged his council-provided refuse and recycling bins the length of his gravel driveway, where he would leave them for collection – a task which even his thirteen-year-old daughter would manage from time to time without injury or incident. But then he started to realise that, more and more, his bins were being missed out so he decided to contact his local council. Nothing could have prepared him for their reply, which stated that health and safety implications meant that refuse collectors could not move the wheeled bin if it was parked on gravel just in case it toppled over and caused an injury. If the Birkett bin was to be emptied each week, it would have to be placed a foot closer to the edge of the kerb to keep the bin men happy.

THE PLYMOUTH BINQUISITION

Forget *Big Brother*, it's Bin Brother that seems to have made an appearance in Plymouth where the city council's policy on waste disposal and recycling has led to some probing questions being asked of its residents. Can you see outside in the dark? Can you push a heavy-wheeled object? How many adults and children live at your property? Do you use disposable nappies? Do you have a medical condition? These are just some of the questions asked in a legally binding questionnaire sent to 50,000 homes as part of the city's plans to reorganise rubbish collections.

But the real cause of uproar from Plymouth's denizens came about after all households were asked to nominate an individual who would be responsible for all recycling and rubbish collections. Now, if a bin is put out at the wrong time, overfilled or contains the wrong sort of rubbish, that person would be liable for a fixed penalty fine or even prosecution.

TRIPLE BIN TROUBLE

It's one thing having to jump through hoops to satisfy local councils and their bin police by placing the right rubbish in the right bin in the right place on the right day, but quite another when you're told you have to empty the bins yourself.

In 2005 Craven District Council rolled out a new and innovative type of wheelie bin called the triple bin. At first glance it looks just like a normal 260-litre wheelie bin but open it up and you would see that it contains two additional 50-litre 'pods'. The main part of the bin is used to collect paper and card, while the smaller units are there for glass and cans. All clever stuff, you might think.

That's what residents thought, until a 2008 health and safety review concluded that, due to the height of the bins, the loaded pods were too heavy for the bin men to lift and were having 'a negative effect on many staff'. The council then wrote to all the householders using the bins, many of them elderly, asking them to remove the pods themselves prior to each fortnightly collection 'to take the strain out of the job'.

Perhaps they'd like the refuse wagon washed while they're at it?

WHEELIE RUBBISH

When residents of a small block of flats in Worcester realised that the bins either side of their properties had been emptied but their communal bin had been missed out they wanted to know why. The answer was simple – the bin had a broken wheel, therefore the bin men were refusing (sorry, no pun intended) to move it.

The situation, however, soon descended into farce when maintenance workers from the same council said they could not repair the faulty wheel while the bin remained full of rubbish. It took a full four weeks to get the problem resolved and then only after the head of the council's Cleaner and Greener department became involved.

Looks like Worcester Council threw out their common sense years ago!

WORKPLACE WOES AND WORRIES

IT MATTERS NOT WHETHER YOUR JOB INVOLVES BATTLING THE HIGH SEAS OR FIGHTING THE OFFICE PHOTOCOPIER — WHATEVER YOUR OCCUPATION, YOU CAN BE CERTAIN THAT THERE IS A PLETHORA OF HEALTH AND SAFETY RULES AND REGULATIONS AT HAND TO SAVE YOU FROM YOURSELF.

A LACK OF FLARE

Flares – not the horrendous 1970s fashion faux pas but the bright, glowing sort – have for many years been an essential tool in maritime rescue. Fired into the air they can provide light for over two minutes at a time – when every second counts, lives are on the line and there is a need to quickly and efficiently illuminate a large area of open sea, nothing else comes close. Of course there are hi-tech alternatives – like night vision goggles and thermal-imaging cameras – but these are costly and can only be used by one person at a time.

It's amazing then that the Maritime and Coastguard Agency (MCA) now consider flares to be a risk to health and safety and have withdrawn them from use, instead saying that each of the 400 MCA crews based around the country should rely on torches or the specialist equipment fitted to the twelve coastguard helicopters that cover the United Kingdom's 11,000 miles of coastline.

Just imagine the difference between finding a tennis ball on a football pitch at night with a handheld torch rather than switching on the floodlights!

A WELSH WIND UP

In 1858, when David Rees's great-great-grandfather, Thomas Davies, became the first official winder of the Llandovery town clock, Queen Victoria was sitting on the throne, Charles Darwin was writing *The Origin of Species* and work was commencing on the excavation of the Suez Canal. Davies was a familiar figure in the Carmarthenshire market town as it was his job to wind the clocks on all of the local churches, schools and other civic buildings.

Over the next 150 years the important function of civic clock-winder remained within subsequent generations of Rees's family, who all took on the role with dedication and enthusiasm until it eventually passed to David Rees. In all those years there was never one mishap, accident or injury.

But now the local council have called time on his activities – apparently ascending a 12 ft ladder and squeezing through a narrow hatch constitutes 'danger under extreme and difficult conditions', with the confined nature of the clock tower making it impossible to install the extensive safety restraints and railings required to satisfy their health and safety officers. For now, at least, the clock has ticked its last tock.

BOB THE VIOLATOR

Can he fix it? Yes he can – although in the process he would probably be in breach of a whole clutch of health and safety regulations and be in line for a significant fine, criminal record or even imprisonment. Bob the Builder, the popular children's TV character, came under fire after the health and the safety police noted seven violations of workplace safety procedures in a single episode of his eponymous show. Amongst his criminal behaviour, Bob was seen to walk underneath heavy equipment suspended from a crane, swing from a bulldozer, drive without using a seatbelt, destroy council property without permission and fail to comply with building site visitor safety guidelines by allowing his secretary, Wendy, on to the site without an EN-397 approved safety helmet – he obviously knows better because Bob's never seen without his! But, rather than being banged to rights and thrown out of the Federation of Master Builders, Bob managed to successfully redeem himself by offering his backing to the Health and Safety Executive's own ladder safety campaign appearing on literature and at trade fairs in the 'flesh'.

COASTGUARD CONUNDRUM

Think about the emergency services for a second. The clue is in the title – emergency. Whether it's the police, paramedics, the fire service or any other department, if you call an emergency service there's a very good chance that you need their help in a hurry. But according to the Maritime and Coastguard Agency (MCA), that shouldn't be an excuse to miss out on a bit of paperwork. Each and every one of the MCA's 400 rescue teams are now required to complete a 'vehicle pre-journey risk assessment' before they can travel by road to an incident.

First it's the simple stuff like the date and time, then they have to provide a reason for the journey (man drowning in shark-infested waters), before detailing any potential risks or delays that the rescuers may encounter (sharks, water, filling in pointless forms) and the actions taken to mitigate the risks (big stick, lifejackets, wastepaper basket). Oh, and they have to include both the current and forecast weather conditions for the day, too.

Perhaps next they'll be asking the victims to sign an indemnity form before they're allowed to be fished out of the water?

IT'S ALL IN THE TITLE

Whatever it is that you do for a living, the chances are you're not a part-time toothbrush assistant. Nor, we could hazard a guess, are you a breastfeeding peer support coordinator, a roller disco coach, a falls prevention fitness advisor, a street football coordinator or even a cheerleading development officer. The truth is, however, that although you might not possess one of these illustrious job titles someone else actually does and they're all employed by local councils the length and breadth of the nation. Add to that a ceremonial sword bearer, a composting supervisor and a befriending coordinator and you'll have some idea where your council tax is going. Now where do you apply for the role of tea dance compère?

Here are thirty more real occupations that have seen their job titles take on a twenty-first-century makeover:

Ambient Replenishment Technician – supermarket shelf-stacker (Safeway)
Cash Relation Officer – bank worker
Coin Facilitation Engineer – tollbooth collector
Crockery Cleansing Operative – washer-up
Dairy Distribution Realiser – milkman

Dispatch Services Facilitator – post-room worker
Education Centre Nourishment Production Assistant – dinnerlady
Ejection Technician – bouncer
Environment Improvement Technician – cleaner
Flueologist – chimney sweep
Foot Health Gain Facilitator – chiropodist
Frontline Customer Liaison – receptionist
Head of Verbal Communications – receptionist/secretary
Inter-home Barrier Installation Specialist – fencing contractor
Knowledge Navigator – teacher
Parking Enforcement Officer – traffic warden
Petroleum Transfer Engineer – petrol station attendant
Resource Operative – handyman (BBC)
Revenue Protection Officer – ticket inspector
Sandwich Artist – sandwich maker (Subway)
Space Consultant – estate agent
Tap and Bottle Supervisor – barman/barmaid
Technical Horticultural Maintenance Officer – gardener
Tonsorial Artist – barber
Vision Clearance Engineer – window cleaner
Waste Removal Engineer – bin man
Wastewater Treatment Officer – sewage worker
Working Platform Technician – scaffolder

It's worth noting that the job of Teenage Pregnancy Coordinator is not as exciting as you might first think.

PC SAYINGS
SEXIST – NON-SEXIST

Craftsman – craftsperson
Disseminate – broadcast
Forefathers – ancestors
Founding fathers – founders
Layman – layperson or non-expert

COMMAND AND CONKERS

Few military forces could be considered as gritty, tough and uncompromising as the Royal Marine Commandos. Formed in 1942, they enacted the famous raids on the dockyards at St Nazaire and were among the first units to hit the beaches on D-Day in 1944. They have seen action in Borneo, Korea, Suez, Aden and were instrumental in the recapturing of the Falkland Islands in 1982.

Being the best doesn't come easy – if you're good enough to get through the formidable selection process you're then subjected to thirty-two weeks of the toughest, most intense and formidable training possible. The pinnacle of your achievement on the way to becoming one of the best of the best would be the completion of the fabled and feared Royal Marines Endurance Course – the toughest seven miles of climbing, crawling, jumping and running in existence.

But, it would seem, even this has come perilously close to falling victim to the overzealous attitudes of Whitehall's health and safety inspectors. After examining all of the obstacles, it was advised that chlorine should be introduced into the underwater tunnel in case some battle-ready commando picked up a bit of a tummy bug. Elsewhere the deep ravines carved by countless army boots into the steep and slippery slopes littering the route were made safer to negotiate – with proper cut steps and the installation of a hand-rail.

At least our Green Berets will be well prepared if they are ever called upon to invade the Alton Towers water slides or a National Trust property.

FLAMING PICQUETS

Join the army, travel the world, meet interesting people… With those very words the Ministry of Defence once sought to encourage the nation's great unwashed to get on their bikes and join up. That was in the 1970s and, although the Soviet Union was seen as a clear and present danger, Great Britain hadn't had a proper war it could get its teeth stuck into for years. The reality was, therefore, somewhat different – rather than travelling the world and meeting people it was odds on that you'd make it to somewhere as exotic as Catterick in West Yorkshire or, if you were really lucky, Bielefeld in West Germany.

Without anybody on hand to shoot at, duties were also often mundane – guard duty, cleaning duty (before it was all handed over to civilian contractors), cookhouse duty. One of the favourite non-duties was that of fire picquet – basically making sure that nothing burnt down. Current Health and Safety at Work legislation recommends that, if you're not actually a trained firefighter, you're not obliged to try and tackle a blaze but, back then, it was all different. Rather like something out of a Spike Milligan sketch, the picquet was equipped with a flammable wooden handcart containing a flammable canvas hose, half a dozen flammable wooden beating brooms and some buckets filled with cigarette butts, chewing gum wrappers and, if you were lucky, some sand. The reality was that this fine array of top quality equipment served only to keep the fire going nicely until some proper firemen turned up who actually had a clue what they were doing but at least then, if duty called, you were allowed to get stuck in and try to do something about it without fear of being reprimanded, sued or sacked.

GIVEN THE PUSH FOR SAVING A JUMPER

For a brave hospital security guard, scaling 15 ft up a scaffolding tower to save the life of a suicidal man seemed a natural thing to do. Having seen the psychiatric patient place a noose around his neck, he gave no thought to his own safety and climbed to his aid accompanied by a paramedic who was also witness to the potentially tragic goings on. The courageous pair were able to hold on to him until further help arrived; they certainly saved the patient's life.

Although praised afterwards by hospital bosses and the police, instead of receiving a commendation from his security company employers, the thirty-four-year-old father of three received his P45 and his marching orders; his actions were deemed a serious breach of health and safety regulations that put his life and the lives of others at risk. Apparently the correct procedure would have been to call the police or fire service and then to wait around for their arrival.

HOW MANY PRIESTS DOES IT TAKE TO CHANGE A LIGHTBULB?

Due to the heights involved it was always going to be a job for the professionals but changing worn out light bulbs at St Benet's Minster in Beccles, Suffolk, always used to be a fairly simple affair. A couple of workmen would pop round to the nineteenth-century church, put up their ladders, change over the bulbs and be gone – all for about £200. But now, thanks to a new directive issued by the EU regarding working at height, seeing the light at St Benet's has become a far more complicated and costly operation involving risk assessments, scaffolding towers and safety harnesses. Replacing four or five bulbs costing less than £1 each can now ring up a bill totalling a rather unholy £1,300.

NO CLEAN SWEEP

There are lots of things you can do when you turn sixteen. With your parents' consent you can get married or join the armed forces. If you fancy a bit of travel, you can apply for your own passport. If you need some transport, then you're old enough to own a moped or even pilot a glider. The world really is your oyster. It is, however, going to have to be a rather grubby oyster because until you reach your eighteenth birthday you're considered too young to clean.

That's what a bright sixteen-year-old A-level student from Chippenham was told after he took on a part-time job with a contract cleaning company. Worried that he could be injured in some freak suction-related hoovering incident, his bosses banned him from using the company Henry and then told him that washing-up liquid, furniture polish and hot water were also out of bounds. He wasn't even allowed to empty the bins. All that was left was the opportunity to wield a mop and wipe with a dry duster. Had he been two years older none of this would have been a problem.

It seems, however, that age is not the only restriction when it comes to being allowed to pick up a broom. Council officials in Edinburgh have banned youth-club workers from mopping floors and clearing up after activities, insisting they would be endangering their own safety as they were not qualified to use cleaning equipment.

NO WAY UP

If you're a driver, in recent years you might well have encountered a SPID on your travels – they're those clever little machines that sit at the side of the road and monitor your speed. Stay within the speed limit and you'll be rewarded with a flashing smiley face;

stray over it and you'll be shamed into submission by a sad one.

For several months, police officers and civilian volunteers in Lancashire had been safely moving, setting up and dismantling the roadside devices using a simple 3 ft ladder without any concerns, incidents or injuries. But according to local health and safety officials, without the use of high-visibility jackets and trousers and a copious number of cones, in bad weather an unsuspecting member of the public might walk into the diminutive stepladder and injure someone. It's not just that – to safely and successfully use such a ladder the user must first undertake a special training course in working at heights and receive the appropriate accreditation.

Perhaps they should just employ taller policemen?

OFFICE BINS SWEPT CLEAN AWAY

Envelopes from the morning postal delivery, the lunchtime sandwich wrapper, the contents of your hole punch – if you work in an office it probably all ends up in the wastepaper basket under your desk. Not if you work for Sandwell Council.

Staff had all of their individual bins removed from their desks and were told to walk to the end of the office every time they have something to throw away. The reason for this is not to promote less waste or more recycling. Nor is it to offer employees a chance for a little exercise during their working day. No, the reason is to prevent risk of injury to the office cleaners who previously had to bend over to empty the offending articles.

PIPE DOWN A BIT

'Its martial sounds can fainting troops inspire, with strength unwonted and enthusiasm raise.' (Henry Kirke White 1785–1806.)

From Mafikeng to the D-Day landings, the skirl of the bagpipe has led many a Scottish regiment into battle. But where massed pipers once struck fear into the hearts of the enemy it's now the pipers themselves who are in the firing line thanks to a report from the Army Medical Directorate's environmental health team.

According to their tests, playing a set of pipes indoors can generate an astonishing 116 decibels and, as a result, trainees at the Army Piping School have been told to pipe down and have had their practice sessions limited to just twenty-four minutes a day outdoors or a paltry fifteen minutes a day if inside. Of course, they're completely at liberty to endure the sounds of the battlefield all day long – or is the army about to put a decibel limit on machine guns and hand grenades?

POLE-AXED IN PLYMOUTH

When the alarm sounds at a fire station, the crew all know that every second can count when responding to an emergency. At that very moment there could be someone trapped in a burning building or an overturned car. Someone's very life could depend on their response time. But at Plymouth's Greenbank fire station rescuers are no longer able to make a quick descent to their waiting vehicles because when it was rebuilt in 2006, at a cost of £2.4 million, a traditional fireman's pole wasn't included in the design.

The reason for this glaring omission remains unclear. At first it was announced that the pole had been excluded due to health and safety worries – perish the thought that a firefighter might twist an ankle or suffer from excessive chaffing – but soon brigade bosses changed their tune, chirruping on instead about how there simply was not enough room for one to be installed. They really must have been tight on space – a fireman's pole takes up only about one square metre of space on each floor. One of the reasons poles have been used since Victorian times is the fact that they are so space efficient. But, whatever the reasons, Greenbank remains pole-less – instead firefighters must clatter their way down two flights of stairs before they can respond to an emergency call – something that even Pugh, Pugh, Barney McGrew, Cuthbert, Dibble and Grub didn't have to do.

STUMPED BY A TREE

When Isle of Mull based engineer Chris Baker was called upon by Scottish Heritage and the Royal Society for the Protection of Birds to assist in setting up a CCTV system, he thought it would be a pretty straightforward job. The task, simple enough, was to fit a special television camera on a tree to assist birdwatchers in observing a rare pair of nesting golden eagles. But just as he was about to make his ascent, watched by a gaggle of officials from the various agencies involved, he was asked if he possessed a National Proficiency Test Council Certificate of Competence in

Tree Climbing. Unaware that such a qualification even existed, he was stopped from performing the simple installation until someone fully certified in the art of arboreal ascent could be brought all the way from the Isle of Skye to assist.

Becoming a qualified tree climber involves completing a five-day training course, for which you have to supply your own specialist equipment including a certified helmet, climbing rope, a sit harness and a packed lunch. Optimistically, you are also required to bring your own first aid kit, an emergency whistle and a knife.

THE OFFICE OASIS

The average modern office can be a pretty faceless environment. Gone are the oak-panelled offices of old, their leather-topped desks and the oil painting of the Director General looking pious and benevolent. No, these days it's all been replaced with a wide open expanse of greyness. Grey-painted walls decorated with the obligatory grey health and safety at work poster. Grey PC monitors balanced on grey melamine furniture in turn resting on a sea of grey carpet tiles. Even the windows, with their thin coating of reflective film, do their best to block out the outdoor colour, ensuring a continued monochromatic state from department to department, with only the lush green foliage of the office pot plants offering any form of visual oasis from the monotonous backdrop.

Often brought in and tended to by company employees, their positioning is usually a matter of personal choice, provided they don't block the fire exits. Not, however, if you happen to work as a civil servant within the corridors of Whitehall. Unable to leave a good thing alone, the Department of Trade and Industry introduced its six-page DTI Foliage Strategy – a 2,000-word triumph of bureaucracy over common sense.

Employees are allowed one plant, 5–6 ft in height, between every three to four seats, but only if the desks are positioned according to the layout specified in the New Ways of Working Scheme. Departments not working to the new scheme are permitted one plant per 120 sq m of UFA (that's useable floor area to you and me). Plants should be placed to create the feeling of an oasis; however, they must not under any circumstances be seen as personal property or moved into cellular offices (that's ones with a door) as this would detract from their benefits to all.

Isn't a bit of greenery meant to reduce stress in the workplace rather than increase it?

HAD AN ACCIDENT AT WORK? NOT YOUR FAULT? CALL NOW ON...

Barely an advert break goes by on British television without some bright spark company of lawyers suggesting that the toe you stubbed on the office photocopier is your key to a cash windfall. Of course it's far from true to suggest that everyone who makes a claim is on the make but these sorts of companies have done more than their fair share of creating the compensation culture that we are forced to live in.

If, however, you're injured whilst serving in the military, it all becomes a bit different – you'll be compensated according to a tariff laid out by the Ministry of Defence Armed Forces Compensation Scheme. Roughly speaking, if you survive a gunshot wound you can expect just over £8,000 for your trouble. Lose an eye and you'll be up for about £29,000, if it's one limb then this increases to almost £58,000, two limbs and you're looking at £285,000. It's incredible to think, therefore, that a civilian RAF typist was awarded almost twice this amount – not for injuries sustained under fire in Basra or from a roadside device in Helmand Province but for a repetitive strain injury in her thumb incurred whilst working as a data entry clerk. Is this classed as a CTRL explosion or RTN fire?

FIREFIGHTERS GROUNDED

With their union bosses citing health and safety worries, firefighters across the land have been told that it is too dangerous for them to climb ladders – an incredible decision considering the fact that ladder climbing forms an intrinsic part of their job description. It's not, however, ascending the 100 ft emergency escape ladders that raises concern; it's climbing up simple domestic stepladders used in helping members of the public with fitting home smoke detectors that's the problem. Although the firefighters themselves are, on the whole, more than happy to continue offering the popular and valuable service, their bosses say that getting them to work 'at height' in a non-emergency situation is putting their safety at risk. Instead, it's up to untrained householders, no matter what their age or ability, to deal with any installations. Of course, should householders fall and injure themselves then the ambulance service will be more than happy to attend and pick up the pieces.

AUCTIONEER HAMMERED

The agricultural world is subjected to a whole litany of health and safety regulations. Livestock auctions are, of course, no exception, especially with the welfare of animals at stake and the potential for the unintentional transfer of disease.

But when Herefordshire auctioneer David Probert received a letter from the Worcester Health and Safety Executive in June 2006 it wasn't the well-being of the poultry sold at his fortnightly auctions that was in question – it was the welfare of his customers' eardrums. With 40 years of sounding the gavel under his belt, Mr Probert was astounded to hear that council officials had launched an investigation into the loudness of his voice.

Threats of further action, however, fell on deaf ears – Mr Probert continued to hold his sales, protesting that if, after four decades of auctioneering, his voice really was a problem there would be a lot of deaf people in Herefordshire.

CHAIR BEHAVIOUR

It's time for a meeting. Including yourself, there are six people attending. You've booked the room, you all arrive and... there are only five chairs. What do you do? Pop next door and get one? Send someone back to their desk to grab a spare? Borrow one from reception? All straightforward and sensible solutions to a pretty simple task you would think. Not if you work in one of the Health and Safety Executive's thirty-one offices.

Employees at the HSE are banned from moving any furniture themselves in case they hurt themselves while doing it. Need a chair moved? First you must book a suitably trained porter to assess the risk and do the moving, and then you'll need to allow them two whole days for it to happen. There are even signs on the walls reminding you not to move things on your own.

Do HSE employees have someone come round and cut up their food for them at mealtimes too?

IN A SPIN AT THE BEEB

When it comes to the subject of health and safety, few of the nation's institutions are known more for their vociferous nature than the BBC. Some of Auntie's activities do require an abnormally high level of risk assessment – perish the thought that it should do something stupid like sending a highly paid television presenter down a concrete runway in a rocket car and have something go wrong – but the corporation seems unable to stop there; even the most mundane and basic of tasks requires evaluation and education.

Staff at BBC Radio Sheffield found themselves issued with a memo on how to correctly boil the office kettle – remove lid, fill with water, replace lid…

Employees at the Beeb's Birmingham studios were sent

illustrated instructions on how to use the newly fitted revolving doors. The snappily titled 'Revolving Security Door User Instructions' advised staff to 'Move directly into the revolving door compartment. The door will start automatically. One person per compartment. Keep hands, feet and bags away from the edges of the door.' Instructing the studio's 800 employees on how to safely negotiate the revolving doors cost an estimated £1,000. It's nice to know the licence fee is being put to such good use.

PC SAYINGS

Motivationally dispossessed – lazy
Niceness-deprived – evil
Parasitically oppressed – pregnant
Satisfaction-deprived – pissed off

THIS LITTLE PIGGY

Bosses at a council office in the West Midlands have banned staff from displaying any pig-related items on their desks in case they are seen to cause religious offence. Items highlighted for removal included a pig-shaped stress ball, a calendar, several china figurines and even a box of Winnie the Pooh branded tissues – because Piglet also featured on the packaging.

NO TIME FOR TAPPING

A department manager, who would tap on his watch every time he saw an employee strolling into the office late, was warned by the company human resources department that his actions could be considered intimidating and construed as harassment.

I'M POLITICALLY INCORRECT AND SO IS MY WIFE

Employees at the United Kingdom offices of a large multinational software company received a memo from human resources advising that, should they encounter any behaviour in the workplace that might be deemed as being politically incorrect, they could, with full anonymity, propose the person involved for a diversity training course. It was then announced that the two-week-long course would be held at the company's training centre in Mountain View, California. A surprisingly large number of employees seemed to have issues regarding political correctness and were subsequently nominated to spend a fortnight in sunny California undergoing social awareness training.

HURRAH FOR THE BLACK SHIRTS!

A telecoms company in north-east England employed a technical support team, all of whom wore green polo shirts as part of their uniform. Within the company it was always known that if you needed technical help of any kind, all you had to do was call the 'Green Shirts'. However, when concerns were raised that this could offend their Indian co-workers, whose national colour is green, the decision was taken to make a change. Suffice to say, little thought was put into the choice of the black polos that comprised the new uniform; no one seemed to have cottoned on to the concept that perhaps a team of 'Black Shirts' would be a less than appealing port of call for help!

HEAR THE ONE ABOUT THE IRISHMAN AND THE SUSPENDED CALL CENTRE WORKER?

Stony-faced BT bosses suspended thirty members of staff at a call centre in Leicester after a harmless Irish joke was circulated by email. Nobody had thought anything of it until a manager began demanding to look at workers' computers to see who had sent and who had received the alleged pernicious communication after a mystery colleague made an official complaint. Incredibly, those suspended included Irish employees who had also forwarded the email to other colleagues.

A WEIGHTY END

Death can be a painful experience in so many ways – emotionally, mentally and not least physically if the deceased's untimely demise was the result of an unfortunate encounter with a runaway steamroller or a marauding bull elephant. Fortunately, compensation culture hasn't quite managed to make the metaphysical leap to a land past the grave; it has, however, found a way to travel all the way to the graveside.

Worried of the possibility that a slipped disc, crushed finger or torn shoulder muscle might lead to a costly lawsuit, funeral directors are now more often than not insisting that any relatives, friends or acquaintances who wish to act as pallbearers first sign a disclaimer indemnifying them from liability.

In some respects, however, it's not surprising that the number of injuries related to coffin-carrying incidents is rising. With obesity ever on the increase, even the size of a standard coffin has increased in recent years – in some cases the combined weight of the remains and coffin can exceed 35 stone (222 kg).

ADULT APPLICATIONS

A position advertised in Scottish jobcentres for a fit and energetic applicant offered a good competitive salary, a thirty-seven-hour Monday to Friday working week in a city location and, with no previous experience necessary, an assurance that full and comprehensive training would be provided. For any prospective jobseeker it looked to be a wonderful opportunity to get back to work – however, a quick glance at the section titled 'duties' soon made it clear that the company involved was not recruiting for a secretary, sales executive or call-centre operator. Not unless any of those roles include 'entertaining customers, pole dancing and private dances'.

The advertisement for a lap dancer to work in an Edinburgh club attracted more than a little attention – much of it from the 'we don't want any of that sort of thing' brigade who considered it to be 'inappropriate'. The advertisement did, however, carry a statement that people were under no obligation to apply for this particular vacancy and that their jobseekers' allowance would not be removed if they failed to make an application.

This Scottish jobcentre, however, was far from alone in offering such positions. Over 2008, a total of 351 vacancies in the adult entertainment industry were offered in British jobcentres. According to the Department of Work and Pensions, among the posts up for grabs were forty-four other vacancies for lap dancers, thirty for adult chat line operators and eight for a topless satellite TV channel. Other more unusual advertisements included requests for a semi-nude butler and a nude cleaner. The ad failed to mention whether a feather duster was supplied or, indeed, what exactly the applicant would be expected to do with it.

SHOULDERING THE STRAIN

We've been warned of eye strain from computer monitors being set at the wrong angle and of repetitive strain injury caused by computer mice. But the latest and greatest workplace injury afflicting the businessperson of today is something altogether different – laptop shoulder. According to research by physiotherapist consultant Diane Hunter on behalf of the Crowne Plaza Hotel Group, seventy-five per cent of business travellers carry their laptop in the wrong sort of bag (supermarket carrier?), with more than fifty-seven per cent suffering from some form of pain or discomfort. So what's going to be the next great executive ailment – BlackBerry thumb or Tweeter's finger?

BROOMS BANNED

According to the Health and Safety Executive, sweeping up wood chippings and sawdust is bad for your health and could provoke asthma attacks or lead to nose cancer. Instead it recommends that joiners and carpenters should invest in hi-tech air purification systems and special state-of-the-art industrial vacuum cleaners which can cost thousands of pounds to purchase and require regular maintenance – a considerable investment compared to a traditional stiff-bristled broom in the hands of an eager apprentice.

ALL POLED UP AND NOWHERE TO GO

Opened in 2000 and costing a cool £235 million to build and furnish, Portcullis House in Westminster is the working home of 210 MPs and 400 staff. Designed to last over 200 years, it features padded lifts, £30 million worth of bronze cladding, electric blinds costing £2 million and a £440 reclining chair for each MP. Oh yes, and a dozen decorative fig trees leased for a five-year period at a cost of £150,000. All in all it's a high-cost, hi-tech work of genius. Surely the designers and architects must have thought of everything? Not quite.

Poor access, difficult light, a maze of ventilation ducts and no provision for attaching essential safety equipment meant that, despite having a perfectly adequate (and probably very costly) flagpole, the annexe to the nation's seat of power was unable to fly a single flag from its roof.

Maybe the government should have asked for its money back?

POLITICAL CORRECTNESS
GONE MAD

STOP AND THINK BEFORE YOU SPEAK BECAUSE EVERYBODY
OUT THERE IS JUST WAITING TO BE OFFENDED – OR, AT
LEAST, SOME PEOPLE WOULD HAVE YOU THINK SO.

IT'S NOT PC TO BE PC

Not so long ago people used to get away with saying or doing things that we wouldn't dream of doing today: Benny Hill would be chased by scantily clad young women; Rigsby would complain about Philip, his well-educated and well-to-do black lodger and Les Dawson would extol the virtues of his mother-in-law. But then came the rise of so-called political correctness and, rightly or wrongly, we were told what we should and shouldn't say.

Kirklees Council took the issue of political correctness to a whole new level by producing a forty-four-page training manual called Equality Essentials, which endorsed PC principals but, confusingly, banned the use of the phrase 'political correctness' itself lest someone be offended. They even managed to suggest that a senior member of the Ku Klux Klan invented the phrase in 1988, despite numerous references to the contrary.

Also on the list of exclusions were the words 'policeman', 'fireman','chairman' and the term 'ethnic', which is described as not being 'appropriately descriptive', despite being the word of choice nationwide for all government bodies.

On a more positive note, workers were advised to create a list of ten things they could do every day to make colleagues feel better. Perhaps number one on the list would be to put the Equality Essentials training manual through the office shredder?

NO BLACKS, DRUNKS OR BUILDERS

Recited by parents and grandparents and taught in pre-schools across the land, nursery rhymes are a perennial favourite. These little ditties, simple as they might sound, often have origins dating back centuries – some are just fun or plain nonsense while others lay claim to more sinister beginnings. Did you know, for example, that 'Three Blind Mice' is a reference to three Protestant noblemen who plotted against Queen Mary I, or that 'Jack Spratt' was about Charles I? The fact that many of these rhymes are as much a part of our literary heritage as Shakespeare, Austen or Dickens has not, however, prevented the PC brigade from trying to change many of the words.

'Baa Baa Black Sheep' has been targeted on many occasions. At one nursery school in Aberdeen the black sheep became a happy sheep, while in Oxfordshire pre-schoolers saw it metamorphose into a rainbow-coloured one – 'to promote equal opportunities' and to ensure that 'no one is pointed out because of their race'. All this obviously pays no attention to the rhyme's thirteenth-century connection to the export taxes on wool products imposed by Edward I.

A national charity dedicated to encouraging children to read decided to replace the 'drunken sailor' in the eponymous song with a 'grumpy pirate'. He's no longer 'put in the brig until he's sober' or 'put in the hold with the captain's daughter' – in the revised version we 'do a little jig and make him smile' or 'tickle him till he starts to giggle'.

But sometimes it's the rewritten version that can get on the wrong side of the politically correct do-gooders. *Three Little Cowboy Builders*, a story based on the classic *Three Little Pigs*, was rejected by the judges of the government-funded BETT Awards due to concerns that the use of pigs raised cultural issues and the reference to cowboy builders could 'alienate parts of the workforce'.

It will only be a matter of time before Humpty Dumpty is on the phone to Claims Direct.

STANDING ROOM ONLY

The students' union at the University of Manchester has caused quite a controversy, having made its toilets unisex to accommodate the needs and desires of its minority transsexual student population. Instead of looking for the 'ladies' or 'gents', those in need of spending a penny now have the option of hunting out either the 'toilets' or the 'toilets with urinals', regardless of what bits they have or how long they've had them.

As you would imagine, not everyone at the university was wholly enamoured with the policy but when questioned as to whether the idea of non-gender specific toilets was 'political correctness gone mad', the union's women's officer just complained that using the term 'mad' was disablist.

NO SAINTS PLEASE, WE'RE BRITISH

In 2004, worried that its name might cause offence to those of differing religious persuasions, Islington Council took the unprecedented and unbelievable step of suggesting that the Saint Mary Magdalene Church of England Primary School should, after 300 years of serving the local community, drop the 'Saint' from its name. With the school due to expand into a city academy for all ages, council officials believed this new name would be more appropriate for Islington in the twenty-first century. But, as parents and local religious leaders from the Christian, Jewish and Muslim communities rallied around, it seemed the only ones with any concerns were the PC-mad councillors who had obviously not done their homework.

With its change of status the school did finally undergo a name change – it's now the Saint Mary Magdalene Academy. Common sense prevails for once!

CHRISTMAS CROSSED OUT

The Yorkshire Coast College in Scarborough, whose motto is 'We Inspire', has removed all reference to Christmas and Easter from its term-time calendar over concerns that those from ethnic minorities or non-Christian faiths might take offence. Christmas and Easter breaks are no more – instead they have been rebranded as 'end of term breaks'. Somebody had better let the non-denominational springtime bunny and the chap in the big red suit know.

Perhaps they had just been taking tips from Oliver Cromwell – celebrating Christmas was banned in England between 1645 and 1660. In those dark days, eating a mince pie on 25 December could get you locked up.

HAP-PC BIRTHDAY GREETINGS

Staff at South Gloucestershire Council were warned that by sending birthday cards containing age-related jokes they could be breaking the law. Calling someone an old git, an old fogey, making comments about their hair blowing north or other parts of their body heading south could be classed, regardless of any harmless intent, as harassment, which is an offence under the Employment Equality (Age) Regulations Act 2006.

MISGUIDED REPORTING

Following the tragic bombings in London on 7 July 2005, the BBC found itself in the firing line for coming up with one of the strangest and most politically correct statements of the year by referring to the perpetrators not as terrorists but as 'misguided criminals'.

Under the BBC's editorial guidelines, the use of the word 'terrorist' is a tricky one to handle – so much so, the corporation devotes over 1,500 words to explaining how reporters and correspondents can convey the horror and human consequence of terrorism without actually using the word 'terrorist', suggesting the use of suitable alternatives, such as militant, attacker, bomber or insurgent.

FULL-ROASTED STUPIDITY

A member of staff (sorry, barista) at a Glasgow branch of a national chain of coffee shops refused to serve a customer a black coffee as they considered it to be racist. Only after the customer had changed his order to a coffee without milk was he able to enjoy his politically correct hot beverage.

BLEEP SAVE THE QUEEN

Airline passengers settling down at 35,000 ft to enjoy an in-flight showing of Dame Helen Mirren's Academy Award-winning performance in *The Queen* could not believe what they were hearing when they realised that all uses of the word God had been bleeped out of the soundtrack. The explanation given was that a rather overzealous and inexperienced employee of the American distribution company had been instructed to edit out all profanities and blasphemies and had got rather carried away.

SCOTS CROSS GONE

A designer working for Glasgow City Council was commissioned to create a circular arrangement of religious symbols to be attached to a set of glass doors in the Scottish Gallery at the St Mungo Museum of Religious Life and Art. As Christianity has been the principal religion of Scotland for many centuries, the designer naturally included a cross in the design, which he chose to locate at the top, only to be told that it would have to be moved so as not to offend non-Christians with its prominence. It was replaced with a Buddhist symbol.

BANNING THE C-WORD

Employees at a company with several offices received a circular advising that, in an effort to respect all faiths and to be culturally diverse, the word Christmas was no longer to be used and that the sending of Christmas cards was banned. In addition, the company's annual Christmas party held in London was replaced with a staff awards presentation but, in deference to its fairness-to-all policy, every office would get an award and nobody would be excluded.

The next announcement in the company circular was a page-and-a-half introduction to Ramadan.

IT'S PAPA CHARLIE GONE MAD

A number of call centres in the United Kingdom have stopped using 'Yankee' and 'Zulu' in the phonetic alphabet for fear they may cause offence, instead choosing to use 'Yellow' and 'Zebra'. Does this mean that they'll have to change 'Quebec' to protect the sensitivities of French Canadians and 'X-ray' lest they offend radiologists?

NO FAGGOTS ON FM

In 2004 a rather creative radio advertising campaign landed supermarket group Somerfield in hot water with broadcasting regulator Ofcom. In the advertisement, a husband is heard to challenge his wife's repetitive cooking routine of a set meal for each day of the week. Protesting, he tells her that he wants lasagne but is rebuffed and told that, because it's Friday, he'll have to have faggots. He responds with 'I've nothing against faggots, I just don't fancy them.'

Despite the supermarket's denials of anything untoward being intended, Ofcom was less than impressed and charged the retailer with breaching Section 2 Rule 9 (Good Taste, Decency and Offence to Public Feeling) of the Advertising and Sponsorship Code.

SHIPSHAPE AND POLITICALLY CORRECT

When fifteen district councillors and seventy council staff from Wyre Forest, Worcestershire, attended a two-day equalities and diversity course run by a training firm from Walsall, they were told that they should not use the phrase 'shipshape and Bristol fashion' as it originated from the slave trade and was used to describe black people who were readied for sale. Similarly, they were told that 'nitty-gritty' should be avoided at all costs because it also has origins in the slave trade – in this case describing the detritus left by the slaves who were transported in the lower decks of ships. However, historians, who many would consider to be a more reliable source than a training company from Brum, tell a different tale.

'Shipshape and Bristol Fashion' is an expression born from the city's strong reputation for ship building in the days of sail. The origins of the latter are less clear but, with the earliest recorded usage being as late as 1956 in the United States, the possibility of being connected with the age of slavery, let alone the slave trade itself, is remote at best.

Thankfully, the enlightened councillors agreed that there would be no change in council policy over the use of these phrases.

YOU ARE INVITED TO A THOUGHT SHOWER

Under instruction from their team of diversity officers, Tunbridge Wells Borough Council has banned the use of the word 'brainstorming' in case it offends epilepsy sufferers. Instead, those involved in generating new ideas will be invited to attend 'thought showers'.

The term brainstorm was first coined in the late nineteenth century by psychiatrists as a way of referring to severe attacks on the nervous system but, since the 1940s, it has dropped into common parlance meaning to think quickly and creatively.

PC SAYINGS
DISABLIST - NON-DISABLIST

Able-bodied person – non-disabled person

Abnormal – different

Crippled – mobility impaired

Handicap – disability

Invalid – disabled person

Mentally handicapped – person with learning disabilities

Mentally ill – mental health service user

Patient – person

Special needs – additional needs

The blind – visually impaired people

The disabled – people with disabilities

Wheelchair bound – a wheelchair user

I'M NOT OVERWEIGHT - I'M UNDER-TALL

When a GP told an obese patient that she was too fat and had to lose some weight or risk serious damage to her health, perhaps even death, he didn't get the response he expected. Instead, Dr Terry Bennett received a letter of concern from local health chiefs after the patient made a complaint against him. Within the correspondence he was advised that doctors were required to be 'professional with patients' and to remember that 'everyone is an individual'. He was then required to write a letter of apology and to attend a training course on doctor-patient relations. He can think himself lucky that that patient wasn't in for advice on cosmetic surgery.

COO NO MORE

You'd have to be a pretty hard-nosed individual not to be touched by the sight and sound of a newborn baby. But, according to officials at Calderdale Royal Hospital in Halifax, saying 'goo, goo, goo' is a big no, no, no. They have banned any and all visitors from cooing at newborns, stressing that it infringed their human rights and highlighted a lack of respect for the dignity of patients. They even went to the extent of putting up a sign reading 'What makes you think I want to be looked at?'

PARTNER ISSUES

When Ian Forrest and his wife went to visit their daughter and her newborn baby at Aberdeen's Royal Infirmary they innocently inquired as to whether her husband had yet arrived, only to be given a severe telling off as 'new mothers do not have husbands, they have partners.'

A PAIN IN THE PROVERBIALS

Collaborating with colleagues at his own place of work, University College Liverpool, and at another university hospital in a different city, Dr David Bowsher of the Pain Relief Foundation spent a great deal of time drawing up a detailed application to the Medical Research Council for funding. The subject of his investigation was to establish differences between 'spastic' and 'flaccid' forms of stroke – terms that have been in use for at least a century.

As the deadline for applying drew near, he began to feel a degree of concern as nobody from the research group in his own hospital had replied to his emails. To his amazement, Dr Bowsher discovered that all of his communications had been stopped in its tracks by an email spam filter because it contained the word 'spastic' – a term which, according to hospital management, was politically incorrect and should, therefore, be banned.

What hope is there for the hospitals and, in particular, clinical research if those making decisions such as these have little or no relevant knowledge and can't even recognise the most basic of medical terms? Unfortunately for Dr Bowsher, this wholly avoidable delay in proceedings led to the grant application deadline passing before he could collate the replies from his colleagues. As a result, he was required to wait a further 12 months before additional funding could be secured.

PAINT OUT THE STARS

Ever since combat planes were first used during the dark days of World War One airmen have decorated their warplanes with morale-boosting comic characters and movie starlets. However, despite there being no record of any complaints from the 5,400 women currently serving in the Royal Air Force, the Ministry of Defence decided that such artworks could be construed as sexist and have the potential to offend female personnel. As a result, the order was given that all military aircraft should be scrubbed clean.

CALL THE POLICE

NOT SO MUCH FIRING UP THE QUATTRO - MORE A CASE OF BREAKING OUT THE BICYCLE CLIPS - PROVIDED, THAT IS, YOU'VE PASSED YOUR CYCLING PROFICIENCY TEST. GENE HUNT WOULD NOT BE A HAPPY BUNNY IN THIS TWENTY-FIRST CENTURY WORLD OF POLITICALLY CORRECT POLICING.

BRISTOL POLICE TAGGED

Graffiti, tagging, street art – call it what you will; with the exception of a few notable examples where the line between spray-can vandalism and truly acceptable art becomes blurred, the idea of someone making their mark with a tin of Halfords' finest does not usually inspire a great deal of support from the general public. No surprise, then, that when a pair of intruders were spotted at a derelict property in Bristol armed with rollers, ladders and enough Dulux to redecorate a cabinet minister's second home, more than a few concerned members of the public were quick to get on the phone to the Avon and Somerset Constabulary.

Once upon a time this would have been a simple arrest for the local beat bobby – a quick 'Oi, you're nicked' and they would have all been off for a visit to the custody sergeant. But things have changed, the proverbial 'risk assessment' is king and it was deemed far too dangerous for a constable to go inside the abandoned building. There was also insufficient manpower available for anybody to wait outside and apprehend the miscreants when they went home for their tea.

Unfortunately for the local graffiti artists the story didn't end there. Just days after the police said they were not prepared to intervene, another spray-can Picasso fell four floors at the property and received serious leg injuries, a broken back, a head injury and internal wounds.

At least the building gained a 30 ft mural of a crocodile and a skull!

A BEAT TOO FAR

Rural crime is becoming a real problem in Britain, with once peaceful villages and hamlets becoming attractive targets for thieves, vandals and confidence tricksters. Villagers in South Cerney and Cerney Wick in Gloucestershire were, therefore, delighted to learn that a new police community support officer, one of the so-called Blunkett Bobbies, had been appointed to keep a close eye on things in their neck of the woods. A visible deterrent is, after all, a powerful thing.

But their first PCSO was a no-show as he was unable to get to the villages under his own steam. At one point it was suggested that he could make use of the regular local bus service but a police inspector quashed the idea, saying the local service had not been assessed for… yes, health and safety.

A month or so later, things looked up with the arrival of a new PCSO – one who could, apparently, either drive or use public transport without the aid of a bodyguard, but delight turned to dismay when, within three months of taking on the role, the new incumbent complained to her bosses that she felt unsafe walking along the village streets as there were no pavements or footpaths. Incredibly, the local police force backed up her stand and said that she no longer had to pound her countryside beat for, you've guessed it, health and safety reasons.

Funnily enough, the local criminal element do not have too many worries about health and safety – burglars are not known for donning fluorescent jackets and graffiti artists never seem too bothered about wearing type TH3 respiratory protective equipment.

DANCING IN THE DARK

Sweaty bodies, a deafening bass, flashing strobes, dry ice filling the air, drink, drugs – it's no wonder that the illegal rave scene attracts young party-goers throughout the country. But while this is all great fun for those dancing from dusk 'til dawn, for local residents the disruption from noise and intrusion can be unbearable.

With police and council switchboards jammed with calls from irate taxpayers one would think the authorities would do all they could to put a stop to proceedings as quickly and efficiently as possible – but no. Apparently it would be a health and safety risk to break up a rave when it's still dark as officers or revellers could be injured. Instead, manpower allowing, the police must wait until the next day and the arrival of daylight before they can intervene.

Perish the thought that a fuse should trip at the local police station and someone would have to sort it out using a torch!

GONE IN 45 MINUTES

Imagine the scene – you leave your car legally parked on a quiet residential street overnight and look out of the window first thing in the morning to see it still there all safe and sound. But then you pop outside just forty-five minutes later and it's missing. What do you do? You get on the phone to the police, obviously. That's how Roger Bugg's morning started when he visited his ex-wife and their eleven-year-old son at their home in Bridgewater. However, Mr Bugg's morning took an even more unexpected turn just fifteen minutes later when the local constabulary confirmed it was they who had removed his car from the roadside and that it had already been crushed – despite the fact that it was taxed, insured and had a valid MOT certificate. But how had this happened?

Bizarrely, a local traffic warden had seen Mr Bugg's ageing Ford Escort, decided that it had been abandoned and ordered its immediate removal on grounds that it posed a fire risk to a nearby electricity substation – because the car windows had been left open, the warden claimed there was a danger that a match could easily have been dropped inside. Avon and Somerset police vehemently insisted that attempts had been made to contact the car's owner in Dartford prior to the crushing but this had been unsuccessful. What a surprise – the owner was in Bridgewater with the car at the time! He had left the windows open an inch or so to prevent the build-up of condensation, which could have caused damage to the tools and electronic equipment that he kept in the car for his work as an electrical engineer. At least with the driver now identified the police could return the coat and sleeping bag that had been recovered from the back seat, but nobody seemed to know what had happened to the tools.

TOUR DE FARCE

Bicycles have been used by police forces in the United Kingdom since the late 1800s. At one time it was a common sight to see a bobby in a blue tunic pedalling his way about his patch. Then along came two-way radios, panda cars and *The Sweeney*, and those bikes were consigned to the storeroom as the whole face of policing on British streets seemed to change forever. Now, a century after the boys in blue first took to the streets on two wheels, pedal power is set to make a comeback; lightweight, rugged and cheap, the mountain bike is the high-speed transport of choice for the modern policeman.

No surprise then that police in Cheshire decided to jump on the MTB bandwagon and invest in a bevy of bikes complete with blues-and-twos. But, like children having their toys taken away on Christmas Day, officers soon found themselves banned from using them – until they had received appropriate training and passed a special cycling proficiency test. This led to a bizarre situation where police community support officers were attending local schools to give advice to children on cycling and road safety but were not actually allowed to ride a bicycle themselves.

TICKETS PLEASE!

A monumental speed camera cock-up cost Dorset police and the local safety camera partnership a colossal £1.5 million. Thanks to the administrative blunder, 24,889 motorists caught for speeding by a single camera over the last ten years have had their fines refunded and points cancelled. The problem arose after the location of a Gatso traffic camera was incorrectly recorded on official paperwork – it should have been in Seatown Road, but was instead located on Duck Street in the small rural village of Chideock. If the paperwork recording an offence is incorrect then it's deemed inadmissible as evidence, leaving every single case open for appeal. The final payout may well be even higher as motorists who received points and were consequently charged more for their insurance policies could be in line for compensation.

ARMED POLICE... PUT THE IPOD DOWN!

When Stoke-on-Trent resident Darren Nixon headed home from his job as a mechanic one January evening, the last thing he expected was to find himself standing at the business end of a phalanx of police with firearms.

His problems started when he reached into his pocket and pulled out his black MP3 player to change track. Unfortunately for him, a visually challenged and easily excited passing member of the public went into panic mode and dialled 999, claiming that they had seen someone take a gun out of their pocket, grasp it with two hands and take aim.

Unaware of the furore that was building, Mr Nixon carried on with his regular journey home – that was until he jumped off the bus and was surrounded by armed officers. After taking out his earphones so he could hear what was actually going on he was handcuffed, bundled into a waiting police van and taken to the local station where his photograph, DNA and fingerprints were taken and he was placed in a cell.

When it finally dawned on the officers that they had not, in fact, affected the arrest of an international terrorist, mafia hitman or Al Capone wannabe and, instead, had in their custody a music-loving car mechanic called Darren, their somewhat bemused suspect was released without charge.

Although innocent of any crime, Darren Nixon's DNA sample and details still remain with the police along with a record that he was arrested on suspicion of a firearms offence.

FAILED

A nineteen-year-old female candidate for the police learned the hard way how important the politically correct issue of diversity awareness is in the modern force. After being put through her paces in the selection process, she was caught out at the last hurdle in a bizarre parody of Gordon Jackson being caught by the Gestapo in *The Great Escape*. She had sailed through her written tests with flying colours but made a fatal error during her interview when asked what she would do if she needed help or advice. Her reply, 'I would go to my sergeant and ask him for help' was an automatic fail – her reference to the sergeant as 'him' demonstrated, in the eyes of the police recruiters, that she lacked gender awareness in her thinking. What a shame to miss out on signing up a bright, young and enthusiastic female officer for the sake of some simple semantics.

THE £2,000 PLAYFUL CUFF

It seems that nobody is safe from politically correct overreaction, not even the wife of the prime minister. When Tony Blair was in power, his wife, Cherie, attended the UK Schools Games at Scotstoun Leisure Centre in Glasgow. On leaving, she was approached by seventeen-year-old grammar school pupil Miles Gandolfi, a talented young fencer from Orpington who was competing at the games. He asked politely if they could be photographed together before putting his arm around her while a friend took some pictures. Joking and laughing, he placed his fingers behind her head in traditional bunny-ears salute. Mrs Blair was aware of his cheekiness and gave him a light-hearted telling off whilst fashioning a playful cuff over the back of his head. Still full of smiles, they parted company and thought nothing more of it.

Unbeknown to either of them, however, one of the organisers from the event immediately contacted officials at the Child Protection in Sport Unit to report Cherie's actions as an assault. The CPSU then passed on details to the Strathclyde Police who despatched a team of six officers to look into the case. Only after the police had spoken to Miles and been assured that he had by no stretch of the imagination been assaulted by the wife of the PM was the matter dropped, although, by this time, the enquiry had already cost in excess of £2,000 of taxpayers' money.

BUY BRITISH? YOU MUST BE JOKING!

When, in the dying days of the MG Rover Group, industry bosses quizzed British police forces as to why they refused to purchase Rovers as patrol cars, one police authority explained that buying 'anything British, including British cars, was an overtly nationalistic statement and could be considered offensive by vulnerable, deprived and ethnic minority groups in our society.' On the other hand, maybe they just like tearing about in Beemers, Mercs and Subarus?

WITNESS FOR THE PERSECUTION

Police in Hampshire called on Jean Grove, a seventy-seven-year-old pensioner, to inform her that the sign on her garden gates was considered 'distressing, offensive and inappropriate'. Quite an amazing discovery considering that the notice advising that 'our dogs are fed on Jehovah's Witnesses' had been in place for the last thirty-two years – save for one occasion when it went missing for a day only to be recovered by a local police officer – over which time nobody, not even the local Jehovah's Witnesses, had proffered a single complaint. The police advised her that a passing member of the public had brought it to their attention.

Although the attending officers witnessed the removal of the sign, a defiant Mrs Grove immediately put it back after they had left.

PC SAYINGS
SEXIST – NON-SEXIST

Man in the street – people in general
Man hours – work hours
Man-made – synthetic
Manning – staffing

POLICE DOG HANDLERS LOSE THEIR BITE

If you think the idea of using a police dog is not only to track but also to scare the living daylights out of criminals, then think again. According to guidelines drawn up by the Association of Chief Police Officers, police handlers are being advised to take into account the feelings of criminals who might be fearful of animals before setting their dogs on them. In addition, they are told to consider the fact that some perpetrators of crime might be allergic to dog hair or suffer from asthma. What are they expected to do, hand out a questionnaire whilst pursuing a suspect across back alleys and garden fences and ask them to sign a disclaimer?

POLICEMAN'S KNOCK

Back in the good old days of *The Sweeney* when Jack Regan and George Carter arrived to 'knock' on the door of some underworld reprobate, the drill was simple – boot, door, a quick slap and 'Get yer trousers on, you're nicked!' Things might have changed a bit over the years, but even in the twenty-first century the technique is pretty much the same – hit 'em hard and hit 'em fast.

Health and safety officials for West Midlands police, however, seem to think that breaking down doors should be a somewhat more technical exercise involving a 'dynamic risk assessment to consider the safety of themselves and others.' Those heading out to administer 'the knock' in an early morning raid are advised to don protective gloves, vests, arm- and shin-guards, thigh protectors, helmets and 'genital protective boxes'. If this is what's required, maybe the officers should be trying to arrest the door rather than the criminals hiding within.

OUR FRIENDS IN BRUSSELS

IT'S COMFORTING TO KNOW THAT DESPITE ALL THE CONFLICT IN THE WORLD, ALL THE WORRIES ABOUT GLOBAL WARMING AND THE DEMISE OF THE PLANET'S NATURAL RESOURCES, ALL THE CONCERNS ABOUT THE ONGOING ECONOMIC CRISIS AND THE RISE OF GLOBAL CAPITALISM, THAT THERE'S SOME HAPPY LITTLE BUREAUCRAT WORKING IN AN OFFICE IN BRUSSELS WHOSE SOLE JOB IT IS TO WORRY ABOUT HOW BENDY YOUR BANANA SHOULD BE OR HOW MUCH A KIWI FRUIT SHOULD WEIGH.

BRUSSELS PIPES DOWN

Church organs across the land came close to playing their own requiem when Brussels bureaucrats sought to implement new regulations limiting the amount of lead that could be used in electrical items to just 0.1 per cent – a good set of organ pipes contain, at the very least, fifty per cent lead in their make-up.

The whole purpose of the regulation was to minimise the level of hazardous waste that makes its way into landfill sites when old and broken electrical products are thrown away. But the ill-thought-out legislation looked set to pull out the stops on the ancient and highly skilled craft of organ building – lead being intrinsic in the construction of a good set of pipes due to its malleability and unique sound properties. New organ orders were put on hold and some centuries-old organs that had been removed for repair or refurbishment were left idling in workshops as it became illegal to reinstall them. The ironic thing about the whole situation is that not one ounce of organ pipe lead is ever wasted – even if a set of pipes is deemed unusable they could easily be melted down and reused. It's a surprisingly green industry – you could even call it organic!

For once there is a happy end to the tale – assuming, that is, that you enjoy the bellowing sound of a church organ in full flow. Thanks to government lobbying an amendment was later granted which excluded church pipe organs from the regulation.

CHEMICALLY CONKERS

Chemicals can be nasty things. Fluorosulphuric acid, for example, is not only highly corrosive but will also explode on contact with water, while tabun, a clear, colourless and tasteless substance, is considered so dangerous it is actually classified as a weapon of mass destruction by the United Nations. In the European Union, all chemicals are required to have an accompanying EU Hazard Data Sheet – a document that lists its potential dangers and advises on special handling precautions.

The records for the chemical BDH 10292 makes for interesting reading. If brought into contact with the skin it must be immediately washed off with soap and water. Contact with the eyes will require thorough and immediate irrigation. Heaven forbid you should swallow some – if this is the case you'll need to thoroughly wash out your mouth and possibly even seek medical attention. Unsurprisingly, the handling precautions for this dangerous substance are suitably strict – rubber gloves and either eye goggles or a face shield being de rigueur, and don't forget the plastic apron and boots if handling it in large quantities. Chemical spills can, of course, be highly dangerous – spill some BDH 10292 and you must mop it up without delay using plenty of water. If, however, you suspect that it has entered any surface drains you must call the local authorities, as they may need to conduct an environmental health inspection. Fortunately, the substance is non-flammable – well, it would be: BDH 10292 is water!

EU DIRECTIVE NUMBER 69?

Whatever it is that you do for a living there's a pretty strong probability that it is governed or standardised in some way by the EU. Musicians are subject to noise regulations, window cleaners are now told how long their ladders can be; you're even told how long you can spend in front of your computer screen before you must take a break. Bureaucrats, keen to make sure that 'best practice' is adhered to whether you spend your working life standing up, sitting down or lying on your back, have even placed the world's oldest profession under the Brussels microscope.

Its booklet, *Hustling for Health*, proffers information on all aspects of prostitution from health and safety guidelines through to the use of an easily recognisable system of stickers that can discreetly notify clients that condoms are to be worn at all times. The 30-page document, produced at a cost of £700,000, also features chapters on working outdoors, indoor work in commercial premises and advertising. In a section offering advice for health workers counselling the profession, it suggests that 'a madam may want advice on how to sterilise her whips.' At least they haven't yet incorporated standardised sizing or weights and measures into the equation.

GIVING BRUSSELS THE BOOT

Thanks to our friends in Brussels, the humble Wellington boot is now classed under an EU directive as 'personal protective equipment' and, as such, must be lab-tested and, unless sold as a fashion item, supplied with a twenty-four-page user manual printed in ten languages. Within the covers of this esteemed tome are sections on risk assessment, storage, life expectancy (of the boot rather than the user) and their resistance to oil. Surprisingly, there is no mention of their use as personal protective equipment against water so don't say you weren't warned if yours spring a sudden leak.

PC SAYINGS
SEXIST – NON-SEXIST

Master copy – top copy
Masterful – domineering
Old Masters – classic art
One-man show – one-person show

FOR COMPETITION USE ONLY

For competition use only – words usually found adorning hi-tech titanium and carbon-fibre components in the high-speed world of motor racing. But now the phrase is turning up in the most unexpected of places – the hallowed marquees of the Scottish Women's Rural Institutes. No, the ladies in the Tweed twinsets have not suddenly decided to pit their wits against the likes of Sebastian Loeb in the Rally of Great Britain; the competitions in question are the traditional cake-baking contests held at fetes and country fairs throughout the summer months.

EU regulations on food hygiene have resulted in the banning of the consumption of cakes, scones and puddings entered in such contests. Under the auspices of the SWRI, all entries must be destroyed immediately after placings have been awarded. To cut down on unnecessary waste it has been suggested that avid bakers submit only bite-sized morsels for judging.

Sheila Gillon, housewives' convenor of the SWRI, was less than impressed with the new mandate. 'I won't be making any more clootie dumplings,' she said.

EU SECRETS OF THE SKIES

The European Commission has been forced to release details of a confidential memo circulated to airlines operating within the EU outlining a series of objects that it considered to be potential terrorist threats. The list, which was used by security staff to prevent items being brought on board aircraft as carry-on luggage, only came to light after an Austrian tennis player, Gottfried Heinrich, was stopped from boarding a plane in 2005 when he refused to put his rackets in the hold. Heinrich took his case to the European Union's Court of Justice, who decreed that it was not right for 500 million EU citizens to be told to obey laws they could not read for themselves.

But what other heinous items of mass destruction were also contained on the top-secret list of terrorist weaponry? Here are some items that appeared on the list:

- ⊘ baseball bats
- ⊘ clubs or batons
- ⊘ cricket bats
- ⊘ fishing rods
- ⊘ golf clubs
- ⊘ hockey sticks
- ⊘ kayak and canoe paddles
- ⊘ lacrosse sticks
- ⊘ martial arts equipment
- ⊘ skateboards
- ⊘ snooker cues

It's hard to imagine an Al-Qaeda cell going tooled up to wreak terror in the skies with a skateboard, a fishing rod and a canoe paddle.

LOST ACRES

First it was pounds and ounces and then it was inches and gallons – thanks to EU regulations, so many of those traditional measurements which have defined British life have now been cast by the wayside. Now another is set to follow.

In Britain and Ireland from January 1 2010, all official documents and advertisements are required to refer to land in metric hectares instead of acres – the ancient measurement derived from the area of land which one man behind an ox could till in a single day. There's something else to mull over with your 568.261 millilitres of beer.

BOTTLED UP

Since he created the Lurgashall Winery on a 38-acre estate nestled beneath Blackdown Hill, the highest point in West Sussex, back in 1985, New Englander Jerry Schooler has built a business that now produces in excess of 400,000 bottles of award-winning fruit wine and mead every year. Celebrated around the world, his wares, such as elderberry port liqueur, rose petal wine and the patriotic St George's mead, are available in many exclusive establishments and are even sold at the Royal palaces. In 2008, however, Mr Schooler was forced into a head-to-head battle with Brussels after West Sussex County Council trading standards officers declared that he was contravening EU Directive 2007/45/EC – meaning his bottles were the wrong size.

For years he had used traditional 75 cl and 37.5 cl bottles but, according to the newly implemented regulation, the smaller of the two sizes was now outlawed – it having been replaced with a slightly smaller 35 cl bottle and a larger 50 cl bottle. To continue production, the business was forced to invest £30,000 in new bottling machinery, new labels, new boxes, new corks and, of course, new bottles.

Despite his American roots, Mr Schooler proudly flies the Cross of St George and the Union Flag outside his winery. Funnily enough, there's no sign of the blue and stars of the EU flag.

FOOD FOR THOUGHT

WHERE ONCE FOOD WAS A THING TO BE ENJOYED IT IS NOW A THING OF WORRY AS MORE AND MORE PERFECTLY HEALTHY INDIVIDUALS BECOME CONVINCED THEY ARE THE VICTIMS OF COUNTLESS FOOD ALLERGIES AND AFFLICTIONS. BE WARNED: THIS CHAPTER MOST DEFINITELY CONTAINS NUTS.

THERE'S SOMETHING FISHY ABOUT THIS

To receive a letter in the post from the local environmental health department informing you that you're the subject of an investigation is always going to be a worry – even more so if you're the owner of a small catering business. But when Steve Moreton was on the receiving end of such a letter it was he who smelled a rat and not the inspectors.

The letter advised him that the council were investigating an odour emanating from the premises' ventilation system. It went on to tell him that the alleged odour was that of fish and chips. This news was hardly a revelation to Mr Moreton – his business is called the New Scarborough Fisheries; it is, unsurprisingly, a fish and chip shop and has, to the best of his knowledge, been smelling of fish and chips for over 40 years.

TOO TALL FOR A CHEAP CHINESE

How tall is too tall for a cheap Chinese? According to a restaurant in Gloucester it's anyone over 140 cm in height.

When the Gardner family visited the city's Angel Chef Chinese restaurant, they were surprised to find that the bill came to more than had been expected. After querying the calculation with staff they were told that, at 149 cm, their ten-year-old son was too tall to be a child and would have to be charged for a full adult meal.

CRAZY DISCLAIMERS

Tesco tiramisu dessert – do not turn upside down

Marks & Spencer bread pudding – product will be hot after heating

Asda semi-skimmed fresh milk – allergy advice: contains milk

Sainsbury's peanuts – contains nuts

A CASE FOR CAKE

There's nothing more satisfying than a slice of cake – especially if it's home-made and served with a lovely cup of steaming hot tea. It's what afternoons were made for.

If you happen to be in or around Humberston Fitties on the Lincolnshire coast over a bank holiday weekend and fancy a slice of coffee and walnut or a serving of lemon drizzle, then there's only one place to go – the chalet of Diane and David Tovey. Heralded for their exceptional patisserie skills, these retired chefs have delighted local taste buds with their home-baked delicacies for several years, with all of their proceeds going to the Royal National Lifeboat Institution. Environmental health inspectors from North East Lincolnshire Council even awarded the couple a four-star rating for food hygiene.

But other council departments were less impressed and asserted that, by selling cakes at their home (even for just nine days a year), they were 'trading' from the premises and contravening their tenancy agreement. Furthermore, the council insisted that the Toveys took out a £5 million public liability insurance policy costing £150 (or about 300 cakes), despite the fact that several insurance companies said it was totally unnecessary.

There is, however, a happy ending to this tale; with support from their MP, national newspapers and the local TV news, the council authorities have, at last, relented and granted the charity fundraisers a special licence to sell cakes on nine days each year – although they're still required to contact the planning enforcement team beforehand. We can only be thankful that the council has enough spare time on its hands to sanction the provision of cakey snacks to the general public!

EGGLESS IN DEVIZES

For fifteen years, the staff, pupils and parents of St Nicholas Primary School in Bromham, near Devizes, had raised additional money for school funds by holding a celebratory St George's Day breakfast in the local community centre. As many as 300 villagers would happily take part, enjoying a traditional fare of sausage, bacon, eggs, tomatoes and toast. But, in 2006, the whole charity event was abandoned at the very last minute when the organisers were unexpectedly informed by local council officials that the frying of eggs could present a health and safety risk.

According to council regulations, volunteer workers are not permitted to prepare or serve 'protein-based foods' without first having received the appropriate training. A licence to grill, you could say.

CHIP TRIP CHALLENGED

For years, residents at the Lakenfields sheltered housing complex in Norwich had savoured a weekly Wednesday fish and chip lunchtime treat thanks to the efforts of fellow resident George Pretty, who would drive to the local frying emporium on their behalf.

But after wardens at the OAP establishment attended an externally run food hygiene course, his chip trips were curtailed. They claimed that because Mr Pretty was not using a special polystyrene transit box to transport the food he was contravening health and safety regulations and putting the residents at risk of getting food poisoning. This was despite the fact that each portion of fish and chips was wrapped in its own polystyrene carton and that his drive back took little more than three minutes.

By the same judgement, this would mean that any of us who popped out to collect a takeaway meal would be at risk of being poisoned – that sounds a bit fishy doesn't it?

UPDATED PLOUGHMAN'S CAUSES FURROWED BROWS

In the days before the panini, the filled baguette and the breaded Camembert graced chalkboards and bar menus across the land, the mighty ploughman's lunch reigned supreme. What finer treat is there at lunchtime than to fill your hungry belly with some thick, buttered crusty bread, a generous chunk of local cheese, a pickled onion or two and a gorgeous crunchy apple?

The ploughman's, however, is under threat. From trendy city bars to traditional country inns, the trusty ploughman's is being ousted by its politically correct cousin – the plough-person's lunch; a dish constructed ostensibly in the same way but frequently blighted by a catalogue of incorrect ingredients. That wedge of traditional cheddar or tangy stilton could be replaced with a decidedly continental slither of cambozola, dolcelatte or buffalo mozzarella, while the freshly made crusty bread might find itself usurped by a strangely shaped focaccia or ciabatta.

The worst, however, has to be the pretentiously titled plough-persons platter available at an eatery not far from this writer's desk – yes, there is the obligatory block of cheese (in this case a moderately sized wedge of cheddar), but it is accompanied by a handful of thinly sliced squares of wholemeal bread, delicate little silverskin pickled onions in their own ceramic ramekin and a small piece of smoked trout. A nice little Kensington snack perhaps, but not exactly the manly – sorry, personly [sic] – fare to see a hardy farm worker through a tough day on the fields.

THE TIP OF THE ICE CREAM

For some it's raspberry sauce and a flake, for others it's chocolate sauce and candy sprinkles. One of the delights of buying an ice cream is choosing which toppings you want and watching your masterpiece take shape before your eyes. Health and safety concerns, however, have forced patrons of luxury ice cream chain Morelli's to participate in a touch of gelato DIY. Fearful that errantly dripped strawberry syrup could pose a serious slip hazard in their bars, staff have been banned from adding topping themselves and are now required to provide all accompaniments from sauces to sprinkles and chopped nuts to fresh fruit in a separate cardboard tub for the ice cream enthusiast to add at their own will.

CRAZY DISCLAIMERS

Happy Egg Company free range eggs – allergy advice: contains egg

Cadbury's Dairy Milk – contains milk

Rowenta steam iron – do not iron clothes on body

Nytol Sleep Aid – warning: may cause drowsiness

ON THE SMALL SIDE

A Bristolian fruit and veg wholesaler, Tim Down, found himself out of pocket to the tune of £1,000 in sales and was forced to throw away over 5,000 Chilean kiwis thanks to EU grading rules after inspectors found that his produce was undersize by just a single millimetre. Despite being perfectly fit for consumption, the thirty one 10 kg boxes of fruit were deemed by the Rural Payments Agency to have failed in meeting the minimum standards for saleability. The rules even prevented him from donating the fruit to a school or hostel – if he had done so he could have been in line for a fine of up to £5,000.

Some other regulations affecting the dimensions of fruit and vegetables include:

A string of onions must consist of no less than sixteen onions, which must be bound together.

A bunch of grapes must not weigh more than 1 kg.

Carrots must not be forked, and must be smooth and regular in shape. If they are less than 20 mm in length, they must be referred to as 'early carrots'.

For bananas, 'the thickness of a transverse section of the fruit between the lateral faces and the middle perpendicular to the longitudinal axis must be at a minimum of 27 mm' – in other words they must be bent to at least a minimum standard.

Class 1 green asparagus must be green for at least eighty per cent of its length.

It's Enough to Drive You Nuts

Whether you're purchasing Christmas crackers or lighting your own camping stove, there's always somebody on hand to abandon common sense and wield a book of rules and regulations. Go ahead punk, ruin my day.

THE DIGITAL REVOLUTION

Unless you've been living in a small closet with only your 14 in black and white Grundig television set for company, you should be aware by now that the government is all set to turn off the analogue television signal and that, by the end of 2012, the only way you'll be able to watch your weekly dose of *Songs of Praise* or the *EastEnders* omnibus will be through a digital set. No problem, we've all been out buying new high-definition TVs and digi-boxes. But did you know that in 2015 the analogue radio frequencies are going to be for the chop, too? The only way you'll be able to listen to your radio favourites will be through the delights of DAB. So this might not be the biggest problem at home or in the office but what about in your car? Motor manufacturers continue to churn out model after model with FM radios when they could be fitting digital sets for the same cost. Ah, but then they wouldn't be able to charge you £300 for the privilege of upgrading as an optional extra, would they?

THE LAW IS CRACKERS

According to the Explosives Act 1875 and the Fireworks (Safety) Regulations Act 2004, it's illegal to sell Christmas crackers to anybody under the age of sixteen – a fact that came as a bit of a surprise to a twenty-two-year-old university student who found herself being asked for proof of age when she tried to buy the festive items from her local Marks & Spencer store and was forced to leave empty-handed when she was unable to provide any photographic identification.

But it's not just Marks & Spencer who are crackers about crackers. Officials at Stansted Airport banned Christmas crackers from all planes because they believed that if one was pulled in-flight, the bang could cause panic – they must be impressive crackers! Another of their concerns was the fact that they could be used to illicitly conceal weapons or dangerous substances within hand luggage. Shouldn't the security X-ray machines be able to spot things like that?

KARMA POLICE

In the Buddhist faith, it is said that the wind chime acts like a divine voice – the mantras cast within are constantly repeated in its sound by the power of the wind, while its clarity of tone clears the mind and soul and assists in relaxation and meditation.

Their motives might have been a little less spiritual, but the feeling of calm created by the gentle tingling of a Tibetan wind chime was exactly the reason that Ryton-on-Dunsmore residents Sheila and David Bavington placed one in the garden of their detached home. Unfortunately for them, not everybody seemed to appreciate the karma it brought to that particular corner of Warwickshire and a complaint was lodged with the local authorities.

After an investigation that cost more than £1,000 of taxpayers' money, Rugby Council sent the Bavingtons an official letter informing them that the inch-diameter chimes constituted a 'statutory nuisance' and they must be taken down immediately or they would be served with a noise abatement notice and be taken to court.

Buddha said, 'Believe nothing, no matter where you read it, or who said it, unless it agrees with your own reason and your own common sense.' Buddha was obviously more than used to dealing with political correctness and health and safety!

A TAXING SITUATION

According to the UK Tax Avoidance Schemes Regulations 2006, it is illegal not to tell the tax man anything you do not want him to know but completely legal not to tell him something you do not object to him knowing. So if you don't mind him knowing that you've not paid tax for the last ten years does that mean that it's not illegal to keep quiet about it?

TODDLERS IN THE HOOD

In an attempt to curb petty crime and antisocial behaviour, plenty of shopping centres and department stores now enforce a ban on hooded tops. For the most part it makes perfect sense – CCTV is only of any use if you can actually see the head of the person you're watching. One corner shop in the city of York, however, seems to be taking the definition of what constitutes a hoodie to extremes. First it hit the headlines for refusing to sell a morning paper to a middle-aged nurse wearing a hooded lambswool cardigan and then, little more than a month later, it made the papers again having instructed a two-and-a-half-year-old boy shopping with his grandmother to remove his hood. Perhaps they were worried he was a rusk addict?

BANGED UP INSIDE

Locked up for five years at Her Majesty's pleasure for a string of charges ranging from deception to obtaining money with menaces, the outlook for Karl Jones, a prisoner at Wayland Prison in Thetford, Norfolk, was pretty grim. That was until an unforeseen 'slip' in the shower landed him in hospital and the Home Office in hot water.

Three years after the incident he sued for damages, insisting that he was unable to work, could not walk without a walking stick and suffered erectile dysfunction – all as a result of his injuries. The details went on to state that he could not remain seated for any length of time, was unable to drive a car, could not decorate his house or tend to his garden and that he now required special accommodation.

Home Office officials buckled under the pressure and decided, in an out-of-court settlement, to award him £75,000 for specialist back equipment, £40,000 towards a new property, £108,000 for care and support and an additional £40,000 for loss of earnings, despite the fact that, by his own admission, Mr Jones had never worked a day in his life; all in all a staggering £248,000.

Needless to say, after the case he looked very happy – as he walked along unaided, carrying his nineteen-month-old daughter in his arms. Now what was he inside for again?

NHS JARGON

Disinvestment – cuts
Indication of needs matrix – waiting list
Performer – doctor
Proof of concept – pilot project
Service user – patient

HIGH-HEELED HOO-HA

In a ridiculous turn of events, a woman from Paignton, Devon, managed to avoid eighty hours of unpaid work she was given as punishment for a series of serious motoring offences because she claimed that, due to a medical condition, she could only wear high-heeled shoes.

While driving her car, convenience store worker Deborah Stallard was involved in a collision with another vehicle but, rather than stopping to exchange details, she fled the scene of the accident. After a speedy investigation, the local police caught up with her the very next day but she then refused to give officers a breath or blood specimen to check for traces of alcohol or drugs. In court she subsequently pleaded guilty and was ordered to undertake unpaid community work, fined £60 costs and disqualified from driving for three years.

The farce, however, commenced when she arrived to carry out her first session of community service, which involved graffiti removal. Probation staff informed her that the less than practical four-inch heels she was wearing breached health and safety regulations and that she must change into flat-soled boots. Mrs Stallard, however, claimed that, after years of constantly wearing high heels, any other footwear caused her pain. Incredibly, when the case was taken back to court, magistrates in Torquay waived her community service order and, instead, made her wear an electronic tag for six months.

NO LETCHERS PLEASE

Are you happy with where you live? Not the bricks and mortar – the actual address. If you live at 25 Acacia Avenue, Averagetown, Boringshire then you've probably given it very little thought, but there are some addresses that can raise more than the odd eyebrow.

When a new street in the Gateshead suburb of Birtley was named, it was supposed to pay tribute to a well-respected local historian who had worked in the pits and lived a humble Quaker lifestyle. The gentleman in question was one Harry Letch. Unfortunately for Harry, residents of nearby Poplar Crescent (could a street possess a more middle-of-the-road name?) were less than impressed at the prospect of having a

Letch Mews on their doorstep and decided to kick up a fuss with the local council, claiming that it was 'obscene' and a cause for embarrassment. The council said that the name had been chosen quite innocently and that none of the three councillors who had passed the decision had given a second thought to the idea that it might be considered to have sexual connotations. Fortunately for all concerned, a compromise was reached and the street was duly renamed Harry Letch Mews, ensuring that the man who put Birtley on the map made it onto the map himself after all.

CONCEALING THE BUTT OF THE JOKE

Twenty-first birthday parties are there for two reasons – to celebrate a coming of age and for parents to cause their offspring the maximum amount of embarrassment possible as suitable revenge for the countless hours, days, weeks, months and years of rudeness, clothes-washing, lift-giving and lifestyle-financing. What better way, thought mother Gail Jordan, than to have a picture of her son David printed on top of an iced cake – especially if the image chosen was one of him as a baby lying face down, displaying his peach-like derriere for the world to see?

The supermarket censors at her local Asda store had different ideas, however, claiming that the proudly displayed bare buttocks could be construed as pornography. Only after the inclusion of a strategically placed modesty star could the cake-topping be printed, much to the birthday boy's relief, perhaps!

TOP DOGS NOT TRUSTED

Sir Ranulph Twisleton-Wykeham-Fiennes OBE is, according to the *Guinness World Records*, the world's greatest living adventurer. He has discovered lost cities, conquered both the North and South Poles on foot, climbed both Eiger and Everest, run seven marathons in seven days on seven different continents and is a man so hard that, when suffering from severe frostbite to his left hand, he amputated his own fingertips in his garden shed using a Black & Decker.

But when he and round-the-world yachtsman Sir Robin Knox-Johnston found themselves working alongside war correspondent John Simpson for the BBC series *Top Dogs*, no amount of real-world experience could protect him from the corporation's vociferous health and safety pen pushers. All three were handed an enormous tome before production commenced warning them of the hazards that could be expected working on a television set – all of which seemed unnecessary considering the fact they were due to film in the truly hazardous surroundings of Afghanistan, the Arctic and Cape Horn.

But the icing on the cake for all concerned came about when the two great adventurers were prevented from lighting a simple Primus stove – something they had done on countless previous occasions in the most hostile of conditions – unless suitable precautions were taken and they were appropriately supervised by a health and safety officer. Fiennes's answer was short, sweet, to the point and not found in any health and safety manuals.

LET'S CALL THE WHOLE THING OFF

A reputable landlady, keen to ensure that her multi-tenanted property complied with all the latest health and safety regulations after the installation of a new boiler, invited her local council to inspect the property. As the brand new boiler had been installed by a council-approved, Corgi-registered plumber she assumed that the process would be a simple one involving little more than a brief wave of a tape measure, a prod here and there and the ticking of copious boxes on a checklist. How wrong she was.

The first to arrive was the council fire officer who objected to where the boiler had been placed and proceeded to order the fitting of two further fire doors. Then along came the local environmental health officer. He had no problem with the boiler but thought that the two new fire doors posed an escape risk – the landlady, as a result, was told she needed to install some new windows with different handles.

The fire officer then returned to inspect the new doors and decided that a gate should be built into the fence at the back of the property to allow firefighters access in the event of an emergency, but when the environmental health officer returned for his second visit, he said this would be unacceptable as people running out to the roadside through the newly installed gate could cause a danger to oncoming traffic.

She never learned what the fire officer subsequently had to say about matters – she sold the property and moved out of the area rather than put up with all the petty bureaucracy and stifling red tape and regulations.

THE LUNATICS HAVE TAKEN OVER THE ASYLUM

In reality, their footsteps may well have echoed through this nation's corridors of power for many centuries but, thanks to the annulment of an ancient and archaic law dating back to Elizabethan times, persons labelled as 'idiots' – those defined as being 'incapable of gaining reason' – and 'lunatics' – those only 'capable of periods of lucidity' – are now permitted to stand for parliament. Whether this will make any improvement to the country's economic state remains to be seen. If nothing else, it will go some way to putting us further in line with our friends in Brussels.

Have you enjoyed this book? If so, why not write a review on your favourite website?

Thanks very much for buying this Summersdale book.

www.summersdale.com